Tarot Reading for Beginners

Tarot Reading for Beginners

The Newbies Guide to Tarot Card Reading and Tarot Card Meanings

Includes Tarot History, Clearing Your Tarot Deck, Major Arcana, Minor Arcana, and Common Tarot Spreads

Shawna Blood

Copyright © 2017 by Shawna Blood

All rights reserved. No part of this publication may be reproduced, distributed, or transmitted in any form or by any means, including photocopying, recording, or other electronic or mechanical methods, without the prior written permission of the publisher, except in the case of brief quotations embodied in critical reviews and certain other noncommercial uses permitted by copyright law.

CAC Publishing

ISBN: 978-1-948489-03-4

Shawna Blood

Table of Contents

Chapter 1: Tarot History 7

Chapter 2: Insight and the Tarot 11

Chapter 3: Getting Started – Clearing Your Tarot Deck . 17

    Earth Element Clearing 20

    Water Element Clearing 21

    Fire Element Clearing 21

    Air Element Clearing 21

Chapter 4: The Major Arcana 24

Chapter 5: The Minor Arcana - Wands 88

Chapter 6: The Minor Arcana - Cups............................. 104

Chapter 7: The Minor Arcana - Pentacles 135

Chapter 8: The Minor Arcana - Swords......................... 151

Chapter 9: Performing and Understanding the 3 Card Tarot Spread... 166

Chapter 10: Performing and Understanding the Celtic Cross Spread 169

Chapter 11: Interpreting the Cards to Tell a Story........ 175

Chapter 12: Conclusion - An Easy Spread to Get You Started.. 176

Chapter 1: Tarot History

Let's review the history of tarot cards first. Some people view tarot cards as part of the occult, mysticism and divination. That couldn't be farther from the truth. The fact is that, originally, tarot cards were used simply to play games. It began with the wealthy upper class in Italy as far back as 1440. And, although you will find many ancient Egyptian symbols on the card, there is no evidence linking the tarot to ancient Egypt.

So, again, they were originally created as a game for the upper-class nobles in Italy. The 22 cards, referred to as the "Major Arcana" were extravagant hand-painted cards for Italian nobility to amuse and entertain themselves.

The three decks originally created by the Italian in 1440 were also known as the "Visconti Trumps", and they are today viewed as the ancient elders of the Tarot. The cards held symbolic pictures such as the Pope, the Emperor, the Wheel of Fortune, the Devil and the Moon. We identify with these same cards in the Major Arcana portion of the tarot decks we use today. The tarot cards at that time were used to play a card game called "Triumphs". Similar to what we know as bridge, it was played with the 22 cards without suits serving as the "trump" cards. The trump cards, of course, outranked the other cards. Triumphs was extremely popular with the ruling and upper classes and spreading quickly through Northern Italy and then on to the East of France. Once it began spreading to other countries, changes were made to the pictures of the trump cards.

During the 16th century, tarot cards were used to compose poems in which personality characteristic descriptions were taken from the tarot. Poets would use the titles of the trump cards to produce pleasing verses to describe the ladies in the court. In addition, tarot cards were used for prophecy purposes where the meanings of the deck were entirely different from today. In 1589, there was one case suggesting witchcraft with the use of tarot cards, but there was no other written evidence of its occult use until the 18th century.

It was then that the tarot was regarded as having mystical and spiritual/occult connotations. But, although tarot cards weren't the norm, ordinary playing cards were linked with divination and the occult as far back as 1487. The first full reference of the trump cards was in a sermon. The reference was made by a Franciscan friar who stated that the trumps were developed by the Devil himself. It was at that time that the use of the cards was condemned and the Devil was accredited with the ultimate triumph of the trumps. He argued that the Devil won through the loss of souls in the game.

In relation to the ancient historical association of the tarot, Antoine Court de Gebelin, also in the 18th century, in France, was convinced that the tarot deck had a linking to Egypt constructed on its imagery.

And, he felt that there were secrets which needed to be deciphered in those pictures. It wasn't long after that where everyone was looking at the tarot as a card system with deep hidden meanings.

The clandestine history of the tarot was again stirred up by the idea that the creator of the secrets was a god named Thoth, also known as Hermes Tresmagistus. This modern occult myth of the tarot began in the 1700s by Antoine Court de Gébelin. He believed that the images contained signs representing Isis and Thoth. He also believed that the word "Tarot" came from Egypt meaning royal and road. His conclusion was that Tarot meant "the royal road to wisdom". He also declared that the gypsies - descendants from Egypt - used the cards for divination initially and were the first as a travelling group to present the cards to Europe, and even though the later Egyptologists could not find anything to validate this, it has endured as part of the tarot legacy.

Moving in to 1781, Comte de Mellet wrote an article on tarot which was published in Court de Gébelin's Le Monde Primitif. He was the first to believe and write that there was a link between Hebrew letters and the tarot cards.

The 19-century famous occultist, Eliphas Levi, established a relationship between the Kabbalah and the tarot. The Kabbalah is also known as Hebrew mysticism. Therefore, this drove the impression that the tarot originated in Israel and contained the wisdom of the Tree of Life from the Kabbalah. This notion brought the 78 cards together into an even key to the mysteries and was passed on to the English-speaking world as a viable form of divination.

Finally, it was author Edward Waite who was credited with the Renaissance of the Tarot in the 20th century. He commissioned Pamela Coleman Smith to produce what he termed the "Rectified Tarot." Waite, a member of secret societies, also joined forces with one of his brothers, an esteemed mystic. His brother, whose last name was Rider, with Waite, created the Rider-Waite's 1910 Tarot Deck. This deck has turned out to be the worldwide standard tarot deck. It was then, and still being now, the most popular deck due to its rich symbolism and ease to interpret.

To get your very own Rider-Waite Tarot Deck, click [HERE](#)

Chapter 2: Insight and the Tarot

We all have a certain degree of what is called insight or intuition. This may or may not comprise of being psychic as well. Intuition/insight is our inborn capabilities to sense things in the world everywhere around us. It is our innate or unconscious perception that has nothing to do with our cognitive aptitudes of reason and logic. Intuition is a gut instinct that we feel notwithstanding what we are sensibly supposed to feel or not based on any particular situation. Insight or intuition warns us when there is danger around. It is the inborn inner sense we have that turns on for specific situations when logic isn't the way to deal with it. For instance, you may meet a person who seems to be very nice, but your intuition instinctively tells you otherwise. That being the case, just be sure to keep your guard up until that individual proves themselves. It usually just feels like something isn't quite right, and our gut instinct tells us that something is wrong. That is intuition.

Life as a psychic is the outward understanding to things outside of what is recognized as the typical range of awareness. It can take many forms. The media always makes it seem like some extraordinary capability to bend objects or move tangible material with our minds. While these marvels do occur and individuals are skilled with that capability; not every psychic can do that. Some individuals possess the gift to hear things, some see things, some are able to channel in the spiritual realm. All of the above are associated with being psychic. Just like intuition; an individual who is considered to be psychic has the skills to inherently sense things. Not all psychics implement their psychic skills the same way. For example, some have such skills as clairvoyance (hearing things spiritually) and others might be telepathic (able to read or hear what a person is thinking or saying nonverbally). Others might have paranormal gifts (able to bend objects or move them with their mind) or supernatural predispositions (see and feel beyond the ordinary range of reason by interacting with spirits). A person can possess intuition and not be psychic, and a person can be both psychic and intuitive.

To read tarot cards, it isn't required that you be psychic, but it is significant to tune in to our insights. However, the more we use our perceptions the more we open up our senses and have psychic flashes as the result. Every tarot card has a standard connotation, but the variance between a good tarot card reader and an average one is how advanced their insights are. An intuitive reader uses their senses and gut feelings together with the precise explanation of each card in order to obtain the complete crux of the cards meaning. As with everything else in life, the more we use our perception the sharper it will become. And, the more solid our intuitions grow, the more precise our readings become. Tarot cards are tools which helps emphasize the intuition for those with innate skills. Some individuals possess intuition as a gift, and others might have to work harder to open that part of themselves in order to have a slight intuition. Many times, individuals with robust instincts to the point of being psychic may have had it in their families, and it was passed along from generation to generation.

Many individuals who aren't open to the idea of tarot cards and intuition dismiss the idea of reading them as a cheap shop hoax. The reality is, though, that most individuals have a misunderstanding of what a reading actually is. It is the intuitive gift that the reader possesses and how he/she applies them to the tarot cards which makes the reading real. Most folks who read tarot cards are already intuitive to some degree when they take it on early in their lives, which is what made them gravitate to the tarot to begin with.

The tarot cards are not magic when you remove them from the box. It is actually the individual's energy that is used to create that magical interaction between themselves and the cards. It is the individual's joining to the cards their intuition and their interpretation which makes the magic happen during a reading.

Just like there are countless forms of tarot card readers; there are also many tarot decks to pick from. When an individual buys a tarot deck, it is typically the artwork which attracts them to that particular deck. An individual will read successfully if they connect to the artwork on the tarot cards. This is due to the fact that the artwork gives the individual a sensation based on what the images mean to them. For example, a person with an American Indian devoutness might gravitate to the decks which are inclined toward the American Indian people both spirituality and culturally because they can identify with the artwork. Thus, the imagery in the tarot cards is heightened by the affinity the individual has to the artwork - culturally and spiritually.

Another thing that is significant for that magic linking to the cards is the life force energy in our bodies. Life force is the energy in our body that circulates through our existence and links us to our spiritual core. It is what gives us will, vitality and a spiritual connection to things outside of ourselves. This energy is set free when we touch the tarot cards. In other words, our energy is conveyed into the cards by simply placing our hands on them. When we use the cards during a reading, our energy streams into the cards from our hands since we willfully direct our attention to the cards.

Readers use this energy in different ways. Some will basically permit their client to touch the cards so that they can feel the person's energy, and other readers will not due to the fact that they don't want to blend their energy with the individual's they are reading. In fact, it is totally up to how every individual reader chooses to work with the energy we have as well as the energy of the individual who is being read.

When we select the cards (and this is true predominantly for veteran readers), the cards transpose an energy through our hands and tell us when to stop shuffling and/or when to throw a card down on the table. There are readers who will use the other individual's energy and ask them to shuffle and pick the cards for their reading. In either case, it is that energy that motivates the individual to select and shuffle the deck for the message they are going to obtain.

The symbolic meaning of tarot cards also varies between readers. It rests on how their perceptions construe and relate to a specific card. For instance, the death card for a particular reader might literally mean someone is going to pass away; and for others it might mean the end of a certain period for a person in life. Therefore, if a person goes to a reader and sees the death card, it does not necessarily mean someone is going to die. It might mean the end of a relationship or routine, or that that person needs to totally change their life. It's really all about how the reader attaches to the imageries in the tarot cards and senses how that relays to the individual being read.

When a person initially begins to read the tarot, there might be misperception about the interpretation of a tarot card. This is when the person's intuition truly is asked to work. When this occurs, it is best to focus all of your care and energy on that card and ask your intuition to inform you as to what that card is saying. Visualize it in your mind's eye, and the scenario it invokes in your mind's eye. This way can help provide you with an explanation to comprehend what message is being given by that specific card.

In addition, it is a great means to grow your insight in relation to reading your tarot cards. You begin by receiving the traditional standardized meaning of the card, and then question your inner self, your intuition, as to what it means. Then, you will begin to assume the energy of the cards and connect it with your intuition. This serves two distinct purposes - it aids in memorizing each card by a standard meaning and then aids in developing your intuition as to what that card means to your senses. Take note of the sensation you get when you do this with each card because the feeling you get is the energy that that card draws on. This is what will make the difference between just anyone reading cards and a good reader. A good reader will be in tune with their energy, the joining they have with the cards and their intuition. These two elements – energy and intuition - are what goes into the cards from the reader to give a vibrant and precise reading.

There are readers who are also channelers. They use spiritual guides to help them with the readings. They are basically individuals who possess intuition and also possess a spiritual element to some degree and their psychic aptitude is able to work in the spiritual realm. They are the tarot readers who invite their spirit guides to come in and assist them when they do readings. A guide is a spiritual entity who helps them. They might speak to them, they might guide their hands, or they might, in fact, enter the reader's body. This, however, is a different facet of a gift that I am not going to concentrate on in this book. Someone who can do this is not a beginner and won't need this book. And, it is not essential for reading the tarot. What is vital is that you are open enough to permit your intuition to work for and with you when you interpret the cards and their meanings

Whatever works for you is what is best. Take the basics and run with them and then read the cards to the best of your ability!

Chapter 3: Getting Started – Clearing Your Tarot Deck

By now you should have purchased your new deck of tarot cards. There is a procedure termed "clearing the deck" that tarot readers perform prior to using the cards. This is completed to clear any negative energy from the tarot deck and to begin to impart your own energy on the deck.

There is not just one way to clear your new tarot deck. When you purchase a new deck of cards, it is suggested that they are spiritually ready and purified so that you can conduct readings more efficiently. You can clear your new deck in quite a few ways. Clearing is meant to spiritually clean and formulate the cards for use. In addition, many readers cleanse their spiritual space and the objects in the room that they give readings in the same manner.

The idea is to work with a deck and space which is clean spiritually, therefore the readings won't be clouded with negative remains from other effects. Spiritual cleanliness is in line with any awareness of godliness one has. Once you clear your cards, you eliminate any touches of negative or blocking energy, and then you will be better equipped to use them to the best of your ability with clean and positive energy. Many readers perform spiritual groundwork such as clearing the space and cards of negativity prior to reading each client in addition to the initial clearing. Sometimes, they also perform small cleanings after the reading as well to be sure any negativity from that reading is removed. Some don't. It's all a matter of preference. Some simply do it periodically. It doesn't matter which way you do it after the initial clearing. Do what you feel is best for you and what gives you and your client the best energy. Similarly, by keeping cards and space spiritually cleansed, you can remove false and inaccurate readings. In other words, you won't have leftover energy from the previous reading.

The tarot cards are, in fact, a method of prediction. All forms of prediction necessitate energy. When you clean your cards and space, you are removing the energetic "remainder" that accrues from reading others or using the cards often. This is even more imperative if you are the sort of reader who permits others to handle the cards. Reading diverse individuals continuously would be a suitable reason to make sure your tarot cards are cleared often. The cards accumulate energy. Clearing is like breathing clean air on them. Some individuals can read without doing anything to a deck, but most want to put their own energy into the cards rather than simply taking them out of the box and commencing. When you clear a deck, you are also charging it with your energy as you start to use them by eliminating any other effects on the cards. Clearing also blesses the deck with your spiritual energy.

Below is a list of all the main ways you could cleanse your deck and the space you use:

- Prayers, Invocations, Vigils
- Singing, Chanting, Music
- Ritual Silence
- Create an Altar, Place Statues, Flowers, Pictures, a Glass of Water
- Use A Power Name
- Incense, Smoke & Smudging

- Special Gestures & Offerings, Moving Within or Outside a Circle, Exchanging Gifts
- Lighting Candles or Burning a Fire
- Fasting or Feasting on Special Foods such as Tea
- Using Power Objects like Crystals, Ritual Amulets, Talisman or Religious/Spiritual Jewelry
- Burying or Unburying
- Tying or Untying
- Washing your Hands
- Breathing Techniques
- Shuffling

Most people begin their clearing by summoning good energy to assist them. They request that good energy clear the deck and space, and also ask the energy for a positive charge. The good energy can take the form of whatever you like, such as a spirit guide, a deceased ancestor, white light, whatever you desire. Some people ask for Gods light and intercession, and this is all based on what God means to you.

Below is an easy invocation to clear your deck or space to begin:

Remember, when using it for space, substitute the word space for deck.

"I bless this deck to bring light where there is darkness. I bless this deck with guidance and wisdom for myself and others for the higher good of all concerned. I bless this deck to enlighten myself and others. May all who use this deck know the love of Spirit and be drawn into the light of Spirit. I devote this deck to serve others with spiritual development, for insight, knowledge and to bring inner peace to all

who seek its wisdom. I devote this deck to the growth of my awareness so that I may be a source of guidance to others."

You can add any words you want or change any words to suit the energy you are using as well as your feelings. Whatever works for you and your beliefs.

When this is done, your cards can be wrapped in a silk cloth or put in a nice bag or wooden box. Some people sleep with their cards under their pillow. Others perform Reiki to keep the cards clean or put a crystal on the top of the deck to keep it charged and cleared when not in use. These are just a few basic ideas on clearing your tarot card deck.

Some card readers elect to do elemental clearing. This consists of using an element(s) to clear the cards. The elements used are Earth, Fire, Water and Air. Below are some basics if you elect to clear your cards by the elemental method.

Earth Element Clearing

1. Bury your deck in the silk or bag in dirt, sand or salt for 24 hours.
2. Spread the deck in a fan shape on a table with a cloth under it and sprinkle sand and/or salt on them for 1-2 minutes. Throw away the sand and salt after that. You can also make a powder by crushing dried herbs and then adding the salt and/or sand if you want. Or, just use the herbs. Suggested herbs are Basil, Lavender, Rosemary, Sage and Thyme. You can also use herbs based on cultural affinity.
3. Rub your deck with either sand or salt for a few minutes.

4. Sleep on the deck under your pillow or mattress.

Water Element Clearing
1. Sprinkle the cards very lightly with water and wipe them off.
2. Mix the water with salt, sprinkle and wipe (teaspoon of salt to cup of water).
3. You can use a blessed water such as holy water to sprinkle and wipe the cards if you want.
4. Use herbal teas to sprinkle cards with and wipe.
5. Expose cards to moonlight, and be sure that they are in a safe/protected spot for a few hours.

Fire Element Clearing
1. Pass the cards over and through the flame of a candle (white).
2. Place the cards on a table with a lighted candle in front of them for approximately 5 minutes.
3. Place the deck near an oil burner with some kind of blessing oil, incense or smudge stick for approximately 5 minutes.
4. Leave cards in the sun for approximately half a day.

Air Element Clearing
1. Pass the deck about 5 to 7 times over burning incense.
2. Smudge the deck with sage or herbs.
3. Slowly and deeply breathe on the deck three times.
4. Put your deck next to playing music for 1 hour.

There are individuals who use the elements with elemental symbols created on their belief systems. I choose to remain non-denominational for the purposes of this book. There is a small "elemental ritual" that you can perform that is non-denominational that you may use when blessing you cards.

Light a charcoal or incense and place it in the east direction of your table. Place a lit white candle in the south direction. Then place a glass of water in the west direction and a plate of salt in the north.

Put the deck in the middle. Drop a pinch of the salt in the water, then pick up the cards, fan them out and place them back, saying as you sprinkle the salt water that you are cleansing the cards with water and earth.

Take the cards and pass them through the incense and say you are cleansing them with air and fire. Leave the cards in the middle until the incense and the candle go out and then put them in the cloth, bag or wooden box you have chosen to keep them in.

Just a few ideas to get you started in cleansing and clearing your new deck. Remember, there are many ways to do it. One last way to clear your deck after a very negative reading or coming across negative energy would be to put them in a leak proof container and bury them for a few days. The earth absorbs the negativity. Cleanse and clear your cards as often as you need to.

Readers will smudge the cards and reading area between readings and keep crystals on top of their decks when not in use. This helps to keep the cards and space spiritually clear. Some tarot readers like to regroup the deck by putting the cards in a specific direction and order between readings. Others clap their hands or use a noise such as a bell, a gong or chimes to break standing energy neighboring them and their cards. Some will use visualization and imagine white light around their cards to clear them of negativity. Some cross their wrists over the deck and quickly uncross them to break any dark energy prior to starting a reading. You can also use the knuckle of your non-dominant hand and hit the cards hard visualizing a white light coming from that hand through the cards. Then pick them up place them to your heart and envision a gold light embracing the cards. You can either pray or say a mantra to rededicate good energy to your cards.

The main thing you want to do is what feels right for you.

Chapter 4: The Major Arcana

The "Major Arcana" are the cards which are thought of to be the heart of the tarot deck. There are 22 of them and they are also known as the "Trump Cards." The Major Arcana portion of the tarot deck represents human life and experience from birth through death. They represent the physical, spiritual, intellectual and emotional characteristics related to humans and the universe.

The trumps are comprised of prototypes of individuals. For instance, a few of the characteristics of the cards in the major arcana relate to warmth and nurturing which deals with a mother figure or a strong, commanding, authoritative figure.

The archetypes are symbolic of real individuals, whether metaphorically or really in a person's life. Each depicts a scene that holds symbolic elements. In most decks, every card is numbered from 0 to 22 in Roman Numerals with one word describing the card. There are, however, some decks which have no numbers or word on top. Some only possess a picture. The original decks did not have numbers or words. It is believed that this is due to the fact that most individuals at the time were illiterate.

The images on the trump cards are immersed with symbolism. Major Arcana cards are associated to a person's higher purpose or have a profound meaning for something which is affecting a person's life. They portray the individual's journey through life, mainly with regard to personal development. They portray the individual's journey from innocence to wisdom.

Tarot scholars believe the system represents the enlightenment a person reaches in their lifetime.

The first card (0), the fool, starts out with decisions to make and he meets the magician (#1) who gives him an idea and then onto the high priestess, and so on down the line to #22. The Major Arcana concentrates on the person's spiritual identity and also provides answers to things regarding day-to-day life such as family, jobs, social relationships, finances, etc. These cards represent some facet of the human experience we all go through in life. They also look at our spiritual journey here in life, our dreams, hopes, fears, joys and sadness. When you begin learning about using the tarot, it is recommended that you acquaint yourself with the Major Arcana before anything else. When you are comfortable with these cards, they will assist you in unlocking the intuition you will use for divination.

When performing readings, you will look at the cards in the upright position and the reversed position. Dependent upon how the cards fall will indicate if they are in a positive or negative aspect. And, simply because a card is reversed does not always make it negative. It depends upon the card's imagery, its connotation and relationship to the other cards pulled. And again, as stated earlier, individuals also use their own interpretations of the symbolism once they get an awareness of what the card represents.

The Major Arcana have been denoted as the 22 keys to life.

Now we will look at the basic divinatory portrayal and meaning of each of the Major Arcana Cards:

0

The Fool

The Ruler: Air

The Major Arcana begins with the Fool. This card is characterized by the #0. In medieval times, the Fool was the court jester. He is innocent in God's eyes and says and does the most inappropriate things and gets away with them. He chooses to do whatever he wants.

Therefore, the Fool is known as the card of new beginnings and making choices. It signifies unmolded potential which is neither good or bad but rather encompasses both good and bad. So, the choice is the Fool's to make - whether to go down a good path or a bad path. In other words, he is at a crossroads.

The Fool Upright

The Fool upright signifies the sort of individual who is eccentric and doesn't care, or listen, to what others say. The Fool simply does what is comfortable. He does not hide from the light. Rather, he is sort of like the light of an innocent child.

This card represents new beginnings, new choices, new experiences and a new direction a person may be considering taking. It can also be a path or choice which is filled with doubt. The Fool is a card of taking chances. The expression connected with the Fool is ***"look before you leap."***

This card also represents a new life energy cycle - energy, force, happiness and optimism, upsetting the status quo of the current state of things by unforeseen events.

The Fool also signifies naivety and impulsiveness. This card indicates that very important decisions need to be made.

The Fool Reversed

The Fool reversed is generally advising not to take risks at the current time. It also advises against hasty decisions, impulsive actions and choices. Upside down the Fool signifies being unwise, gambling, uncertainty and wasting artistic energy. When appearing in reverse, The Fool is saying that it is not a good time to make any commitments. It shows that the person likes to start things but tends to never finish what they start. You will also find that this card generally points to an individual who is continuously changing their location and job.

I

The Magician

Ruler: Mercury

The #1 is the number for creation and individuality. This is what "The Magician" is all about; the power to change through the use of his will. The Magician takes the nothing, such as the Zero of the Fool, and changes it into the #1. The Magician is the channel of a higher power. He is also an illusionist and is able to create the illusion of reality by sleight of hand and trickery. He is only confident in the skills he possesses in order to bring forth the results he desires. His true power comes from sources outside of himself, much like in a magic show - there are folks behind the scenes who make it happen. Without these sources, he is powerless.

Magician Upright

When the Magician appears upright, it is cautioning about opportunity which is available to us if we can manage to pull all the pieces of our life together to make it happen. The Magician upright says that the more prepared we are for the change, the better it will be. It speaks of the individual mastering the material world. This can be done through organization, creative action, self-discipline, and an inclination to take risks.

This person having the reading done more than likely has the gift of speech and is able to easily sway people if the Magician card is pulled. He/she should learn to recognize their potential and use their power to initiate things.

This person is witty, has very good communication abilities and can accomplish anything they set out to do.

Magician Reversed

When the Magician card comes up reversed, it means the person is a bit of a perfectionist. They might seem outwardly able to handle any situation due to their cool and calm demeanor; but inside they are uncertain and unprepared. They sometimes use their gift of words to manipulate people. It also could mean this person is someone who abuses their power and uses it for negative purposes.

The Magician reversed show a person who may be disorganized and chaotic. They do not make decisive choices. They like to waver instead of choose. This person is not capable of properly utilizing their time and talent. Individuals who are characterized by the Magician in this position are more than likely lacking inspiration and energy. These people give up easily, have a poor self-image and less than good coordination; and, at times, possibly learning difficulties.

II
The High Priestess
Planet: Moon

The High Priestess is a representation of spiritual enlightenment. She sits between a palm and pomegranate tree which are symbols of male and female energy. Her crown possesses the full moon, and she embodies every virgin goddess.

The High Priestess Upright

Together with spiritual enlightenment, she also signifies inner-illumination and the connection between what is seen and unseen. She is the feminine form of balance and power. When she appears in a spread, the High Priestess is telling you to use your intuition or that you have good intuition. She also signifies that the unconscious mind and inner voice is attempting to give you a message. When she appears, it means hidden knowledge or information will be exposed or that there may be information which is hidden that needs to come to the light. She characterizes hidden truth and concealed inspirations at work.

If the High Priestess comes up in a man's spread, she signifies the woman of his dreams, the love he has been waiting and hoping for. In a woman's spread, she signifies the qualities that the woman either wants or has. In any event, she is saying that something is yet to be discovered. There may be duality and mystery connect to a situation or individual. The High Priestess proposes that there are unseen influences that affect the home and work of that particular person.

High Priestess Reversed

In the reverse situation, the High Priestess represents apparent knowledge and facts. In other words, any decisions you make will be based on facts and logic as opposed to intuition. It sometimes means there is a lack of balance and harmony because of inadequate foresight. It also means that the feminine or instinctive side of an individual's personality might be suppressed. Reversed in a woman's spread means she has a problem coming to terms with either another woman or themselves. It also signifies surface knowledge and/or repression or ignorance of true facts and feelings. Sometimes it can mean being self-centered and/or sensual pleasures contingent upon what is next to it in the spread. It can also indicate that circumstances are not what they may seem.

III

The Empress

Ruler: Venus

The Empress card signifies the epitome of the Earth Mother. Her shield, which is heart-shaped, possesses the symbol of Venus. The Empress is the Goddess of Love and Fertility. She is also known as is Venus and Aphrodite.

Empress Upright

The Empress upright signifies fertility and bounty. Her power embodies creation. She generates life in all ways. As an archetype, she embodies a mother. Motherhood, pregnancy and nurturing are the characteristics this card brings to the spread. She also characterizes everything created in nature. The Empress, just like a mother, represents unconditional love. She represents abundance, material wealth, creation, infertility and artistic expression. This card upright may also signify the sanctuary and steadiness that comes from years having a wonderful marriage or union.

When she is revealed, it may designate an individual who is way too protecting or an individual who is loving kind, gentle, and sophisticated. This card can mean the birth of a child is close in the future. It can also specify that you need to be open to unconditional love. The Empress card, for artistic types, may be saying that they need to cultivate and grow their artistic expression. It is a card promoting well-being and security. This person is creative in finances, love and parenthood. The Empress upright specifies a person who is maternal in nature as well as domestic stability.

She shows accomplishment in goals and growth. Depending up the other cards in the spread, it can also mean marriage.

Empress Reversed

The Empress Reversed shows trouble in paradise or domestic conflict. It can also indicate that an issue within the home is arising from infertility and/or finances. The reversed Empress shows a lack of affection, either given or received, and lack of accomplishment. It can indicate a creative block, issues in a person's relationship, an unwanted pregnancy, abortion, infertility, promiscuity or sterility. The reversed Empress sometimes indicates poverty and trouble with children. It's time to think about what is causing problems in the home.

IV

The Emperor

Ruler: Aries

The Emperor signifies power. The Emperor possesses power through intellect, as opposed to the High Priestess who has power through knowledge.

The Emperor Upright

When this card is pulled upright, this is a person that is in control. Nothing will stop him/her. He/she was born to lead and will dispose of anyone in their way. This card indicates success. If in a good position, it may signify the achievement of goals and ambitions. The Emperor has a commanding presence as he sits on his throne. The number on his card, 4, signifies stability and foundation. The Emperor signifies control of the material world. He is law and authority. He can also characterize a paternal figure and a powerful one at that. This card can also signify someone who is sexually controlled.

Those who have the Emperor show up in a spread are competitive and influential in how they implement things and how they advance them as well. This person is commanding and the Emperor, for them, can signify world power. Through experience, they have gained self-control and are very powerful individuals who can definitely shoulder responsibilities. Their motivations lead them to long-term success.

The Emperor Reversed

Reversed, it suggests that the individual is emotionally immature and may be incapable of leaving home. He/she can't separate from his/her parents. In reverse, this card signifies a loss of control. It also displays that the individual is inactive and does not take appropriate action but rather is passive. They either lost their place of authority or they do not like authority at all, to include a loss of authority in a governmental position or parental authority. In addition, they do not care for the government or do not care to become a parent.

There are indecisive with a weakness in character. And they tend to manipulate colleagues and friends. In reverse, it can also mean an abuse of power.

V

The Hierophant

Ruler: Taurus

The Hierophant signifies the Pope. This is due to the fact that this card represents the presiding influence of religion and faith. It signifies the traditional traditions that are appetizing to the commonalities. This is the difference to the High Priestess who only teaches those individuals who are secretly initiated to her mysteries.

The Hierophant Upright

When the Hierophant turns up in a reading upright, it shows that the person being read has a partiality to a routine of ritual and ceremony. It signifies spiritual power through an institution. This card symbolizes the church or a certain belief system. It might also signify harmony of politics or public opinion.

The Hierophant shows that the person accepts authority. It's a card of conformism about safety in numbers and social pressure. When this card appears, it shows that the person being read desires approval from others. The person may have a desire to conform or is only happy when he/she has societal approval. It also signifies proper education. The individual is a pursuer of knowledge and wisdom. They either give or get good sound advice. This individual can be good at teaching and is a helpful councilor.

It also signifies marriage and partnerships that are bound by ethics. The Hierophant is all about a world with law and order. This person prefers the delusion of security at the expense of freedom. Therefore, if this card is in a good position, it signifies a good and safe standing in society. It can also mean that this individual has the capability to undermine and escape authority contingent upon the spread.

The Hierophant Reversed

If the Hierophant shows reversed, it signifies an individual who is open to innovative ideas and thinks outside of the box. He/she is unconventional. It might characterize a rebellious individual, a hippie, or an artist who colors outside of the lines. It also shows that the individual is at the stage in their life where they need to do something totally changed or outside of their own limitations. Or, when this card is reversed, it can mean deceptive and/or bad advice, poor direction, defamation and propaganda. It's a cautioning to be cautious of initial impressions. There is a misrepresentation of the truth. It is also not a good time to sign contracts, and signifies deceptive advertisements.

This individual is eccentric and does not have family values because he/she rejects them. It can also show a loss of public standing and the overthrow of uniqueness by an institution.

VI

Lovers

Ruler: Gemini

In this card you will find two lovers upended in harmony. They are both nude, which means that they hide nothing from each other. The image infers that somebody has to make a decision whether or not to pursue temptation. These individuals know that in order to possess success in their lives together, they must have a sense of balance between their subconscious and conscious desires.

The Lovers Upright

This card in the upright position says that we have choices to make. It also says that we are human and that we fight ourselves among holy and wanton love. Because of this, it also signifies the steadiness between the inner feelings and outer facets of our lives. This card also represents harmony and union. It says to choose with your heart and not with your intellect. The lovers also signify tough choices not connected to love.

It's all about a test that we may be going through in connection to bearing in mind our promises. It can also signify a struggle between two paths, intellectual thought and accord, inner accord and union among two individuals. The lovers show yearning, a new lover, relations, physical desirability, love, sex and obligation. This card speaks to us about duty vs. our heart's wishes. It speaks of how the choices we make affect the rest of our lives. The Lovers card also says we maybe should take a risk which would lead to fulfillment rather than taking the easy route in love. It also tells us that when a decision is made, if the person stays loyal, they will receive the same in return.

Lovers Reversed

When the Lovers card shows up reversed in a spread, it means that there is a possibility of a poor choice made. It also means arguments and unfaithfulness in a relationship.

The reversed Lovers card tells us we need to calm our emotions and get in touch with our balanced selves as opposed to our carnal selves. Reversed, it also proposes desire, ethical failure, enticement, indecisiveness, separation, an unsuccessful love affair, and emotional damage. Reversed lovers can mean that a person is in an unhappy relationship and doesn't know what to do about it. There is inconsistency, dishonesty, division and internal conflict. It is speaking of unfaithfulness and romantic conflicts. The individual is uncertain and delays decisions of their choices. It also cautions that it is not a good time to make any ultimate decisions on a significant matter. Lastly, you are being untruthful to your own ethics.

VII

The Chariot

Ruler: Cancer

The Chariot tells of riding thru our hardships in victory. The Chariot card means that you are fighting your way thru your battles without giving up.

The Chariot Upright

The Chariot Upright in a spread tells us that our struggles are going to end in triumph. This card instructs that continued hard work and perseverance will result in an ultimate win at the end for you. It tells of your self-reliance and belief in your capabilities. It can also signify unanticipated good news as well as travel and change. Contingent upon where it appears in the spread, it could mean a new vehicle is on the way. Therefore, the card will mean victory, movement, self-belief, confidence and good news. You will overcome the obstacles you are facing at this time.

This person is decisive and determined to achieve their goals, and the victory they earn is deserved. This person has experienced a long period of struggle which will result in success. It indicates self-control, determination and perseverance. The Chariot tells of how this person works well through the limitations life has placed upon them and builds a positive presence through those limitations.

The Chariot Reversed

When the Chariot reveals itself reversed, it tells of a person who is either influenced by a bully or themselves are a bully, conceited and self-centered. It can signify frustration because matters have not turned out the way the person would have thought. It also shows a delay in travel and/or plans contingent upon its position. Plans are not going well. This individual has disrespect for others, and is connected to jealousy and greed. The Chariot reversed shows the individual has lost control of their life resultant in bedlam due to flaws in their personality. Imbalance and destruction. Reversed, the Chariot cautions of overwhelming motivation and very high expectations. Depending upon its position, the Chariot reversed also speaks of outdated ideas and traditions

VIII

Strength

Ruler: Leo

The Strength card speaks of strength in all the ways the notion of strength is articulated by Man. It portrays a man together with a lion and they are in accord, representing that strength does not automatically mean the exhibition of brute force, but rather a sensible display of control and understanding the beast within us. The man in the image is capable of petting the lion, indicating that strength is comprised of the use of tender inspiration in order to achieve the results needed in your life.

Strength Upright

Strength. Not just in the bodily sense; but also, the individual has the capacity to handle enormous pressures, and will win as he/she fights to the end. If bad health is at issue with the individual, this card shows a fast recovery. The Strength card also advises that any unhealthy behaviors should be stopped now. Strength upright specifies victory in the focal things in life. You will win the challenges with regard to relationships or career. It shows that the person can defend themselves against jealousy, ignorance and cruelty. The individual has courage and self-control. The individual has the quality of resilience. He/she is strong-minded. This person can also control their emotions against straightforward instincts. They control both strength and power. The individual has energy, is generous, optimistic and shows steadfastness and understanding.

Strength Reversed

Strength in reverse infers that the individual is self-doubting and fearful. The individual gives up easily due to being beaten in the past by unfair means. It tells of an individual who uses their power in the wrong way and defeat will be involved. There is a lack of will power. The individual feels inadequate about something. They also have a negative attitude with regard to things going on around them or in their life. There is an inclination to surrender to worthless desires.

The Strength card shows oppression. There is a concern involved in the circumstance. The individual has an inability to act on things. In this position, the card also speaks about being cautioned not to miss prospects that are available. Also, it's speaking about the individual not giving up when they are close to the finish.

IX

The Hermit

Ruler: Virgo

The same as an actual hermit, the Hermit isolates himself living a life of isolation, secluded away from the world. You will notice the lone hermit with a light to guide him. This is the light of man's spiritual self-shining as he walks alone.

The Hermit Upright

The Hermit upright means either the individual is living as such or needs to take notice to the wisdom of the Hermit and slow down.

When he appears, he represents the need for watchful reflection of matters. It also suggests that the individual is in need of rest; as well as peace and quiet. If there is a health consideration, the Hermit says that it is a time to rest and recuperate. This card signifies self-examination and seclusion. The individual is looking for internal and spiritual answers as direction, advice either given by the individual or taken with patience. The individual is in need of carefulness and forethought as well as discretion in their life. There is an inner calm.

This card can also show a need to reach one's inner resources. It can also mean adjustment and preparation. Counsel is either given or received to the individual when we see the Hermit. The individual is either a sensible guide or spiritual guide or has one. It is time to reflect on surroundings. The Hermit cautions about making hurried choices and recommends that if a choice is required; make it only after taking direction from a reliable source.

The Hermit Reversed

The Hermit reversed means the individual is impatient which leads to bad decisions and, in turn, lonesomeness. It also suggests that this individual is egotistical and stubborn. The individual is distrustful or creates doubt with his/her behavior. He/she also refuses to regard advice to help him/her. Reversed can also mean anxiety and foolishness as well. These individuals refuse advice or assistance. He/she is immature. It shows some kind of seclusion from others. This individual shows negative resistance to help. The individual's suspicions of others are not grounded or sound with considerable explanations in relation to an individual's motivations. It infers impulsive actions or decisions. There is a continuance of corrupt behaviors and lifestyle that is not fruitful. The individual depends on their own resources which are not suitable. Finally, this individual's stubbornness is irrational.

X

The Wheel of Fortune

Ruler: Jupiter

The Wheel of Fortune symbolizes help from a higher source is on its way. The Wheel of Fortune is round, representative of one cycle ending and another beginning. If we apply this to our lives when we are down, like a circle, we will rise. When we hit rock bottom, we have to come back up.

The Wheel of Fortune Upright

When the Wheel of Fortune appears upright, it is saying that we are about to start a new life cycle. It foretells good luck and fortune. It also infers that it is chance that has brought luck and prosperity; rather than your doing. This card announces the end to existing problems and rewards for past hard work. The Wheel of Fortune card has a karma element to it - fate is smiling on those who deserve it after they have paid for their trials and tribulations. It is a card of destiny, drive, ideas, good luck, a new life cycle and synchronicity. When it shows up, it is speaking of natural achievement. It can also indicate unanticipated good luck. It's a card of progression.

Again, it is a card of destiny in regard to ones Karma and Karmic change.

The Wheel of Fortune Reversed

Reversed, we can expect some unanticipated bad luck. It shows that our fortune is spinning in the reverse direction. It foretells bad luck and unkind surprises. However, sometimes the negative cycle it brings is brief because the wheel is always turning. Contingent upon where it shows up, it can mean; difficulties, momentary bad luck, unpleasant surprises, unforeseen disruptions, complications, postponements and/or a resistance to change. It is also a caution not to gamble.

XI

Justice

Ruler: Libra

The Justice card displays the sword and the scales of balance being held by an individual of royalty. The card represents justice and all its inferences, that justice is served through law and order. Balance is required in order to serve justice. When there is no balance, injustice is prevalent.

Justice Upright

When the Justice card appears, that's exactly what it indicates. That justice will be served. It can also signify that the individual is fair or that a fair decision will be made on the individual's behalf. It suggests balance and symmetry. Justice is a sign of good luck in partnerships, businesses and legal transactions.

It can also indicate the righting of a wrong. It is a karmic card. Those who do wrong are punished by justice. The Justice card rewards for past hard work. Justice may indicate mediation, fairmindedness and accountability. It can show harmonious and promising resolve of conflicts. It represents victory over bias and prejudice. Depending upon where this card shows, it can also mean legal action, lawsuit, agreements, settlements, break up, and sometimes even marriage in conjunction with other certain cards. But only when marriage contracts such as pre-nuptials, legal documents or financial documents are required to make the unification happen. It is a card of precision and a candid choice.

Justice Reversed

Reversed, obviously, it represents injustice. It can also symbolize a business that struggles and legal decisions that will not go your way, even if you are ethically right. The person may be giving or receiving bad advice which will result in a bad judgment. It may also mean prejudice, partiality and inequality.

It can specify separations that are not yet sanctioned or legitimate.

Justice in reverse can mean postponement, postponement on judgments, disproportion, or a discriminating judgment. There may be complex discussions taking place with regard to misunderstanding surrounding a legal matter or tax affair.

XII

The Hanged Man

Ruler: Neptune and Water

We see a man hanging by his foot from a tree. The man does not seem to be in anguish, but is in a situation where he can't move at will. The Hanged Man is a card of limits. Like the hanged man, we are required by circumstance to accept our position. There is a brief postponement of growth, which is also a form of indeterminate state that the Hanged Man can take.

The Hanged Man Upright

This card upright is a card of self-sacrifice. It can take the form of either material or emotional self-sacrifice. The individual may be in a state of limbo similar to what the image shows – a man hanging from a tree facing a gap in life until the individual gives something up for the greater gain. This card denotes a trial of passage, and this is where self-sacrifice arises. It also has spiritual implications with regard to one self-sacrificing themselves.

It also means acclimating to shifting surroundings. In that regard, it can mean change, flexibility, reawakening, deliverance and release. There is dedication to an earnest cause. The Hanged Man may also suggest flexibility of the mind and a readiness to adjust to changes. It shows that there is a sacrifice being made currently to reap the benefits later. There is more than likely a period of waiting for this individual.

It shows a sacrifice of one thing in order to gain another. A card of transformation. It can also show sickness, stress and anxiety. However, this card says that this is the time for patience and no worries.

The Hanged Man Reversed

In reverse, the Hanged Man is saying that the individual is selfish or is using emotional extortion by playing the martyr. It also shows there is a weakness with this individual. And, their weaknesses can lead them in the wrong direction materially and emotionally which will result in missed opportunities. There is a lack of commitment. The individual is preoccupied with material and egotistical needs.

Notwithstanding problems, they still favor the status quo. It can show domination as well as indifferent quest of goals. There is a failure to act with a failure to move forward or grow. There is a stagnancy with this individual.

XIII

Death

Ruler: Scorpio

Most people get frightened when they see this card because they think death is on its way. In reality, the Death card seldom truly means death. It can, but most of the time does not mean physical death. When Death displays itself, it's a sure conclusion and a sure new beginning.

Death Upright

Death in the deck is all about eventual transformation. The Death card can mean outrageous or unanticipated changes and/or events, but it foreshadows these things as being removed to clear the way for a new life. "Out with the old and in with the new." A whole transformation.

It can also show extensive changes. It signifies that the change is the product of your fundamental circumstances which is what produces the transformation. Major change is arriving. It can also characterize that a specific phase of life has played itself to the conclusion, and its purpose was served, an abrupt and wide-ranging overhaul of circumstances, way of life and patterns of behavior due to past events and circumstances. It also warns of disputes.

And lastly, for some, death means an actual physical death.

Death Reversed

Reversed, this card is showing that a person is fighting the unavoidable changes that are required in life. It represents inactivity. Reversed, it's saying that you are missing prospects because of your refusal to let go of the situation. It can also signify fear of change and a loss of friendship. A reminder that transformation is painful and unpleasant for this individual. The individual refuses to face fears of change. Reversed, the death card embodies inactivity and exhaustion as well as mental, physical and emotional collapse.

XIV

Temperance

Ruler: Sagittarius

Temperance is about moderation. When we use moderation, it brings spiritual well-being. Temperance can also signify a person's guardian angel watching over them. This card is saying that this individual either has or needs self-control in their life. If they practice control, they will be able to handle unpredictable situations, and be successful. This card expresses a harmonious relationship together with peace and harmony to be enjoyed. Temperance can also signify health, conciliation and serenity. It can also mean a good mixture, collaboration and synchronization of efforts. There is an innovation through the mixture of either individuals or circumstances. It is also a card of peacekeeping and fruitful business negotiations. There is a sure volume of maturity that the individual has or desires in order to deal with something. This individual has a good-natured, stable personality and good attitude. Accurately, this card means temperance with regard to harmony and balance. The Temperance card foretells good management and the capability to adapt to fluctuating circumstances.

Temperance Reversed

Reversed, it is saying that there is over indulgence, lack of forethought, intolerance, battle and squabbles triggering domestic conflict. It cautions that hurried decisions made out of impatience prevent the individual's progress. Upside down temperance indicates a disparity either with the individual or situation they are in. This individual or situation is heated and they, or the one they deal with, fly off the handle easily because of it. There is lack of good judgment together with indecisive decisions. Inconsistent interests are present. There is physical stress with the individual involved.

Differences are predominant. There is an edginess and unpredictability of the individual or party involved. Depending on where it falls in the spread, it is telling that attempting to combine too many things or the incorrect fundamentals in a short time span will not work.

XV

The Devil

Ruler: Capricorn

The Devil card it is not automatically evil like Satan, but rather the negative characteristics of bodily man. He represents the wishes of the flesh, and such compulsions and enticements under his influence will not have an advantageous result.

Devil Upright

With regard to relationships, when the Devil shows up, he is cautioning us about obsession or individuals that are not good for us. This card is warning you to look at the state of affairs very cautiously. The Devil cautions against damaging consequences as a result of a person's actions which have been driven by gluttony, envy and/or power. The Devil is not necessarily all a bad premonition; he prompts us, rather, to change our course of behavior. He is also telling that if you have any addictions, you should intentionally be aware of how they are hurtful to you and others. This card is beckoning that you need to gain control over those addictions ASAP.

What is interesting about the Devil card is in the upright position, if marriage or commitment is present; then that is a good omen. So, in a positive sense, the Devil can signify commitment and stability. Depending on where it falls in the spread, it could mean money matters and a sense of burden with regard to the material facets of one's life. It shows the individuals longing for physical and material things. This card can also infer the individual has feelings of defeat and domination.

It can also mean the individual has a propensity to collect and hoard both money and objects. This is a card of lust and sexual fixation. It also questions a person's security at the expense of their artistic or spiritual contentment.

The Devil Reversed

Reversed, it also has a dichotomy of meanings. It can mean that there is light at the end of the tunnel with regard to a lengthy struggle. It can signal that problems are being lifted or contingent upon the rest of the cards can show true evil. Reversed, the Devil speaks of abuse of power or authority. This individual is so fixated on material success that they forget about all else. It can signify unrestrained ambition also. Greediness and/or oppression either to an individual or circumstances, emotional black mail and more severe forms of the above are portrayed by the Devil in reverse. We are looking at something, or someone, really evil, contingent upon the immediate cards.

XVI

The Tower

Ruler: Mars

Together with the Death and The Devil cards, The Tower causes us to be scared when we see it in a spread. This card is about unanticipated disturbances, unanticipated surprises and unanticipated events which turn our lives upside down in order to create new opportunities and make us a tougher and wiser individual.

The Tower Upright

The changes that happen when the Tower appears this way are typically abrupt and gives us a shock. Contingent upon where it falls, it can also signify complications and postponements with things such as purchasing a new home or things related to the Homefront. It signifies oppression and rebellion. The Tower characterizes the defeating of your current way of life. Whether the foundation of our being upset is material or emotional, this card inspires you to see the discourse as something to power you into a new and improved direction.

The Tower can also mean this is a phase, and it will pass so a new direction and prospects can develop.

The Tower embodies disturbance and misunderstanding. It's a card of key changes in life and can also mean an abrupt violent loss.

Contingent upon where it falls, it can seem to mean disturbance of a routine at the end of its course. When we see this card, it is telling us that it is time to stop performing the same old things. It can foretell devastation, conflicts, dramatic turmoil, extensive aftermaths of actions and/or a change of job and dwelling at the same time. At the end of the towers cycle, liberty and clarification is transported to the one going through the Tower phase.

Now is the time to reevaluate things. This change is essential and better will come from this chaos. It's really a blessing dependent on the other cards in the spread.

Tower Reversed

There isn't a big difference in the Tower reversed, but that the cycle is coming to an end. Reversed, the Tower is telling that it is just about time to start rebuilding. Reversed, it can mean negativity. It shows there are restrictions and some kind of incarceration, whether it be physical, emotional or spiritual.

The Tower reversed can also mean that there are radical changes that are robbing the individual of their freedom of expression. It can also mean insolvency or jail; literal imprisonment. The reason for the imprisonment can't be changed at the moment. The individual will have to do the time. The reversed Tower can also mean abrupt changes that a person cannot control.

The Star

XVII

Ruler: Aquarius

When the Star is pulled, it's a bright light to brighten our ways. It's, more or less, a welcoming sign. It's a card that is saying if we look to our personal star, blessings will come.

The Star Upright

The Star upright conveys optimism, hope, renewal of faith and surprising gifts. The Star card is one of good health. If the person is considering a new relationship or initiative, this card is a good sign. It basically tells of good things. It can mean good times for the individual with regard to artistic or educational happenings, travel, mindfulness or spiritual growth. It is positive and representative of big-heartedness, tranquility, new hopes and rejuvenation. When you wish upon a star, your wishes do come true. Contingent upon its position, it speaks about healing old wounds and of spiritual love. The individual is expanding their mental and physical horizons.

The Star is also a card of protection. It is telling you that you are safe. The Star shows inspiration. The individual has the aptitude to influence others.

The Star Reversed

Reversed, it shows self-doubt. It cautions us that self-doubt ruins our possibilities for new opportunities. It can also mean poor heath or illness. This person is stubborn. They are either reluctant on unable to adjust to changing environments which stops them from seeing the opportunities that change will bring. These individual lacks trust, in themselves and others. Contingent upon where this card falls, it can show this individual is undergoing impediments to their happiness. Reversed, it can signify a weakened life. This individual has trouble articulating themselves and their mind is inflexible.

Interestingly, even reversed, this card can bring luck notwithstanding the individuals cynicism. Make lemonade out of lemons.

XVIII

The Moon

Ruler: Pisces

The Moon is a card of emotions that run high and feelings of confusion in the form of indecision and anxiety. Like moonlight, it is also a card of illumination together with unforeseen possibilities. It also tells us this individual has insight and there are things surrounding them that are not true to the eye.

The Moon Upright

Contingent upon its position, the Moon can mean a secret affair, but in the upright position, it is a promising sign for that relationship to be able to develop into the public eye. If it's not in a good position, it can mean that the secret may be uncovered. It also signifies the unconscious mind and the imagination. This card means the individual has psychic awareness and dreams of spiritual perceptions. It also means that this individual should listen to the meanings in their dreams and look to their inner voice for illumination on something you are feeling emotionally.

The Moon can also infer the individual performs psychic and spiritual work. This Moon is a card of illusions. It could be telling us the individual is incapable of seeing things clearly which results in depression. It also says the individual is not in control of their daily living situation. But even if the going is rough, the Moon does light the way for you to take the correct path. Contingent upon where the Moon is in the spread, it also foretells of artistic capabilities such as writing or music, and that using those artistic talents can lead to surprising opportunities. It's also promising to those in the acting and entertainment industry.

The Moon Reversed

Reversed, the Moon tells of lack of growth because of deep-rooted fears and worries. It also infers the individual lacks courage in regard to a situation. It cautions of lies and deceitfulness which may be the source of worry for the individual. It indicates either they are lying or they feel someone is not being honest with them. Overall, the Moon reversed is an embellishment of the upright inferences in a reading. Contingent upon where it lies, reversed shows there is a need for silence. There is a ruse, deception, and the individual daydreams to escape from truth.

It also advises the individual has trouble distinguishing make-believe from reality. It also tells of disingenuous individuals, hidden forces and deceit. It suggests the individual has trouble telling the truth because they are not capable of it. In reverse, it is saying this individual is distressed and in need of help.

XIX

The Sun

Ruler: The Sun

The same as we feel happy on a sunny, warm day, so is the blessings of the Sun card. It speaks to all the good things that we have in life and that there is more to come. This is certainly one of the best cards in the deck. It is the most welcoming of cards foreshadowing signs of joy and happy times.

The Sun Upright

The Sun can predict holidays, good news regarding kids, and even the birth of a much-wanted baby. It ousts negativity and promises things will turn out happy. It proclaims happy times with family, friends, pleasant companions and relationships. We should know that we are going to be satisfied, happy and obtain the success we have been desiring.

Contingent upon where it falls in the spread, it can mean substantial prosperity or happiness and good health. The Sun is about mental, emotional and spiritual vivacity. It also implies happiness, enlightenment, fulfillment and love. Also, it could mean you are an inventor with inventions worth sharing. The Sun also indicates academic success, particularly in the field of science. It is a card of reward, praise, approval, wealth of energy and achievement.

The Sun Reversed

Reversed, the Sun is simply telling us there is trouble with arrogance and slipups are due to an overblown ego.

XX

Judgment

Ruler: Fire and Pluto

This card shows that of Karma being judged by a higher power with regard to our fate. The Judgement card shows that what we reap in life, we will also sow.

Judgment Upright

The Judgment card upright speaks of all our hard efforts finally being rewarded. We should take heed of our lives up to this point. It is beckoning you take into consideration a new phase of your life. It suggests if an individual has had bad health that recovery is now in effect and also gives the individual a new lease on life. The Judgment card brings with it a prospect that you should accept. That prospect may come in the form of a decision or project, but it should not be overlooked, because it will change your life.

When in a spread, it shows that things in our life will start speeding up. It signifies a rebirth, time to celebrate, new potential and rewards for past hard efforts. It is a card of transformation and development.

It also suggests a pleasing conclusion to a precise matter or period in life. When we see this card, it is speaking of experiencing joy in our accomplishments. Contingent upon where it is in the spread, it also speaks of awakening. A good time for career moves. A period of mental clarity. It can also mean that an imperative decision that was pending will change our life for the better.

Judgment Reversed

The Judgment card reversed means there is inactivity around us. There is a postponement with finishing a series of actions. Contingent upon where the reversed Judgment card shows up, it can infer the individual has fear of change and sometimes a fear of death.

With regard to the other cards it appears with, it can also mean fear of almost everything in this individual's life. There is lack of advancement in this individual's life due to a lack of significant decision making on their part. One can also experience brief loss or separation when Judgment is reversed. Guilt is also implied when the Judgment card is reversed. There is a sense of self-reproach with this individual and stubbornness. Judgment in reverse cautions about self-doubt and guilt over past mistakes which tends to blur the way forward.

XXI

The World

Ruler: Saturn

This card confirms that the world is at your grasp. All you need to do is stay positive.

The World Upright

The World upright says that you are about to receive your heart's desire, including such things as accomplishment, appreciation, success and victory. The world indicates a time of delight, which can take the form of a vacation, travel or time with loved ones. It means a rewarding relationship is being presented to you along with spoiling yourself with the material things you desire. The World also means the end of one cycle for another. It is a card that tells of contentment, achievement, gratification, joy, completeness and success.

This card signifies a finalized personal cycle, project or series of events or completed chapter in one's life. The World can also signify a culmination of events. The individual has a sense of totality.

The World Reversed

Reversed, it means the postponements you are facing are tests you have to overcome in order to succeed. It also means that you should not give up when so close to winning. It also infers not to lack vision or feel uncertain because you will soon be successful. Reversed, it shows the individual is unfulfilled.

Contingent upon the spread, it shows postponements to conclusion or that there is an incapability to bring things to a positive conclusion. It also suggests the individual is impervious to change and lacks trust in the process. The reversed World speaks of inactivity, lack of will and annoyance with the postponements and hesitancy. It also proposes that the events are nearing the end.

This is the Major Arcana and the meanings for the twenty-two cards. There are many other variations and descriptions to add to these interpretations. As you grow and progress as a reader, your interpretation of the cards will be fine-tuned for your type of readings.

Chapter 5: The Minor Arcana - Wands

Now let's take a look at the Minor Arcana. The Minor Arcana consist of 56 cards. It is broken into 4 suits; each suit having 4 court cards. As you see in the previous chapter, the Major Arcana, also called the Trump cards, deal with the important issues we face in life. The Minor Arcana deal with commonplace issues that we face every day and tell us the best way to handle them. Each suit helps us with a different aspect of our daily lives.

Wands

The Wands, also known as Staff's and Batons, signify fire, the southern direction and summer. The Wand cards deal with primordial energy, progress, will, inspiration, purpose, strength, creation, intellect, imagination and insight. In our daily lives this card characterizes our career paths. Wands mystically reflect what is central to you in your inner being.

Embodied by the element of fire, Wands specifies all the things you do during the course of a day that keeps you busy, whether at work, at home or at play. Wands show ideas, development, motivation and expansion. They also characterize our original thoughts and how they affect our lives. If there are a lot of wands in a reading, that may indicate the conditions in which the individual finds themselves are based first in thought; and then as ideas.

These fire signs are connected to the wands; Aries, Leo and Sagittarius.

The physical characteristics of individuals with regard to this suit are: fair skinned, red to blond and light brown hair and blue, green or light eyes. Also, if you see the 4 of wands it may mean 4 weeks.

Ace of Wands

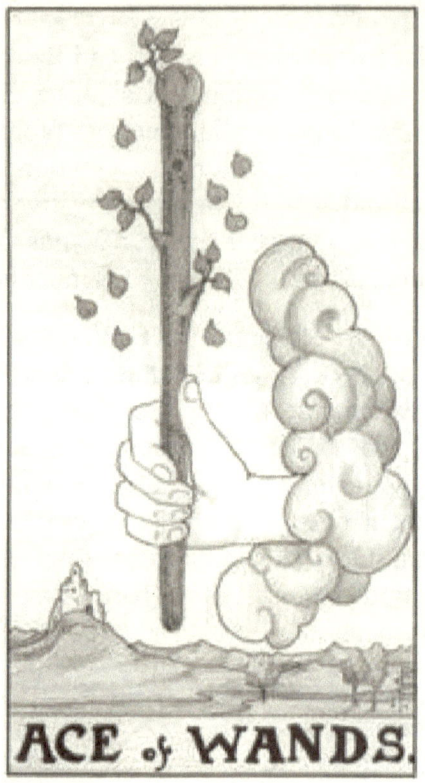

The Aces signify new beginnings. They show ingenuity, determination, potential, and the initial stages of an endeavor.

II of Wands

Twos carry messages of a sense of balance and opposition. When a Two comes up in your reading, you can't move forward until balance is reached.

III of Wands

Threes mean communication and relations. They designate the impact that others have over your life, work, and emotions.

IV of Wands

The fours in a reading characterize a break or resting period. If you want to move forward, you must stop now and consider where you have been, and where you are going.

V of Wands

The fives show hardship. They specify struggle, loss, and other damaging experiences in your life which need to be overcome.

VI of Wands

Sixes signify growth, overpowering challenges, leaving bad circumstances behind, and gaining a better understanding of who you are right now.

VII of Wands

The sevens teach that you need to have faith in yourself and the universe. There are several things happening to you, but self-assurance, willpower, and truth will see you through.

VIII of Wands

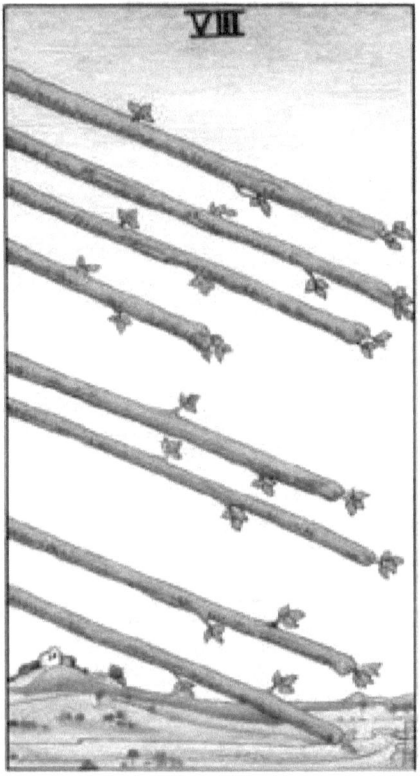

The eights are cards of work and change. They tell you that the only way to get where you want to be is to change what you're doing right now.

IX of Wands

The nines characterize culmination. Things are coming together, and you may or may not like what you see now.

X of Wands

The tens are all about ultimate results and the end of an existing cycle. They convey messages about the rewards or penalties you will experience for the amount of work you have contributed.

Pages

The Page cards signify messages and new beginnings. The Pages show a new stage where you know what you want to do, but not how to do it. These cards say that you need to gather all the info you can before you take your next steps.

Knights

The Knights are all about drive. You know where you are heading, and the Knights tell you that it is time to set the wheels in motion.

Queens

The Queen cards are feminine messages of influence, potential, and guidance. These cards often counsel you to pursue the help of a wiser, more knowledgeable individual.

Kings

The King cards flex their strengths with authority and total control. They basically say that you definitely have what it takes to prosper, but you need to have faith in all that you are.

Chapter 6: The Minor Arcana – Cups

Cups in the Tarot deck embody water, the West and Autumn. They have to do with love, sentiments, moods, choices, concluding stages in one's life, compassion and family life. The Cups deal with the sensitive level of awareness. Cups reflect your impulsive responses and your typical responses to circumstances. Cups have a like-mindedness with religious groups or institutions.

The individuals characterized by the Suit of Cups are commonly fair, plump individuals who are expressive, creative, caring and artistic. They are said to match the water signs - Pisces, Cancer, and Scorpio, and water as a sign of the unconscious mind and reason. Cups are connected with anything emotional, from marriage to personal possessions and worries. This also means anything with regard to partnerships, either work or personal.

If a reading is largely "cups", then you can be sure that the individual is looking for answers to mainly emotional battles, love matters and emotions.

Ace of Cups

Meaning Upright

The Ace of Cups signifies the home and overall atmosphere.

There will be joy in your life with the fulfillment of all your determinations and wishes. Tons of joy will be found in your serenity. This card foretells that you are searching for clearness, or for the truth in a state of affairs where your heart says one thing and your brain another. Or, it can mean you hope an idea will become real. Your ideas will become successful. There is a chance for a marriage either through love or a business partnership and likely a new agreement.

Positivity is in the air, and it is time to forgive and make amends. This is a peaceful time in your life, so use it wisely and make peace with friends or even yourself. It is also a time of fertility and/or child bearing. Maybe an adoption ought to be considered. The Ace of Cups portrays the rise of spirituality and the emerging of a new consciousness of spiritual life. Bliss and supreme happiness are yours if you open yourself up.

The Ace of Cups is a sign of an emotional surge, power of thoughts, promising sexuality, appealing to another, spiritual love or psychic capability, art, first love, intimacy, lover, bond, rejuvenation, water of life, relationship, stimulation, growing, foster, wealth, contentment, harmony, nourishment, safety, weakness, sensitivity, satisfying, goodwill, fertility, compassion, creation, higher calling.

Medically, this suit denotes the Urinary (kidney and bladder problems) and Reproductive Systems.

Reversed

Reversed, this card signifies the sense of when we are about to burst with swarming emotions, either through laughter or tears.

The reversed Ace of Cups is consequently the opposite to the feelings of joy brought by the upright Ace of Cups.

It may be calling on you to control your emotions for your own greater benefit.

On the other hand, the Ace of Cups could advise that you have suppressed your feelings too long, and it is now the time to release them. You might have kept your enthusiasm quiet about the prospect of a new job, in fear of it failing, but now is the time to let those emotions go free. Or, you may have become almost void of feeling true emotions.

This individual is tentative to receive matters of the heart. Reversed, it is representing the worst - a time of desolation; physically, emotionally or both.

II of Cups

Meaning Upright

The II of Cups shows partnership, engagement or friendship. This card is telling of marriage, romance, passions and emotions. The individual will experience love and harmony with sisters and/or brothers, especially if they've had a falling out in the past. The II of Cups displays the beauty and power that is fashioned when two come together.

Commitment is also linked with the II of Cups. It indicates a union, a partnership or an engagement.

This card can also signify the resolution of opposites now in shared trust. Cups propose instinctive and emotional aspects. It could propose a likely new friendship or a renewed relationship.

Reversed

Reversed, it is telling us that something is not in balance. There is a troubled relationship, divorce, mix-up, lack of trust, irrational expectations, break-up, separation, untrue friend, hostility, unreciprocated love, disharmony, incompatibility, loneliness, suppressed rage, arguments, emotional pain, deceived confidence, disenchantment.

Contingent upon where it falls, it can specify a loss of balance.

It also proposes some kind of hang-up concerning the basic message, maybe hesitancy to expose your feelings.

III of Cups

Meaning Upright

The III of Cups is a card of festivity and achievement. The three young maidens dance in a circle with their golden goblets raised in a toast of enjoyment. The III of Cups specifies the conclusion of problems in the past. A conciliation will be made which will serve all the best interests of those involved. There will be time to relax after the conciliation is realized.

The III of Cups tells us that we must change internally, and will want to revise our attitude and the way we deal with what is going on.

What you choose will be the right choice. The number 3 characteristically proposes the preliminary conclusion of a project. Though, notwithstanding the conclusion or gratification presented by the number 3, this card also proposes a new beginning; the celebration is only the start of a long and perhaps tough journey.

It foreshadows boundless joy as a result of a birth or marriage.

The three of cups is a card of bountiful fertility, trust, harmony, maternity and the healing of problems.

Reversed

In association with relationships, the III of Cups reversed almost always shows a third individual is involved.

When you see this card, look to the other cards in the reading also.

Reversed, it can specify that the individual self-indulges to excess. Self-centeredness and sexuality is also implied. Loss of happiness, loveless sex, uncontrolled passion, scarcity and sickness related to smoking and/or overeating are all likelihoods.

The reverse III of Cups also cautions against obesity.

IV of Cups

Meaning Upright

The IV of Cups shows a time of doubt and a turning inward to discover the truth one is searching for.

Outside stimuli can be disrupting and may not lead us to the goal we seek, even if those influences seem to be of a divine nature. The IV of Cups means discontent with someone. You might be tired of the same old fight that has been carried on too long. The conclusion might contain disappointment in the end result.

This card indicates a pause. Dissatisfaction. Monotony.

The IV of Cups proposes the individual re-evaluate their life, because familiarity breeds contempt.

There is a need to hunt for a more inspiring way of life.

This card can also mean the start of creating a family.

<u>Reversed</u>

Reversed, it is suggesting a new relationship is now likely. There is a longing for work and achievement and new goals. There is a good likelihood that a proposition is on its way, but you have to work hard. You might be missing an opportunity that is right there! Look around you to notice the opportunities you might have missed.

This card also tells the individual that their ill health and fatigue is because of overindulgences. In reverse, the IV of Cups can also mean excesses of all kinds.

This individual is completely upending his/her present lifestyle.

V of Cups

Meaning Upright

The V of Cups signifies non-attainment of anticipated results. You may lose something; however, it is irrelevant.

You'll be totally burned out and want to quit. You'll feel like you've done enough and don't want to do anymore. You and a relative (or friend) will soon part ways, and you will be very unhappy.

You want a friend or lover to reappear in your life. Or, in the interim, a real relationship which is based on tenderness and shared attraction. Nothing less. Something will replace the emptiness you feel. This card foretells of sorrow and/or loss of a loved one. The individual's marriage is on the edge of ending.

This card urges you to stop crying over spilled milk and look in a different direction to obtain happiness. Get over the hurt, and carry on.

This card it is telling us to re-evaluate our priorities.

The V of Cups signifies uncertainties and regrets.

Reversed

Reversed, it is telling us of the return of hope and new coalitions formed.

The reversed position tells of recovery from remorse and an acceptance of the past. Now, the individual understands the full insinuations of the past and appreciates the lessons he/she learned.

This card is about learning to be open and starting to take risks again. It is a card of a persistent sense of remorse, reminiscence and sentimental memories. However, the card speaks of being hopeful for the future.

In reverse, it signifies a way of life being turned upside down. Contingent upon the spread, it can also tell of false starts as well as unforeseen worries from a surprising source.

VI of Cups

Meaning Upright

Remembering. It suggests thinking of another by giving a peace-offering or a gift. This card talks about the past and memories. It foretells the individual is looking back. Meeting with a childhood friend.

This card also indicates new surroundings and opportunities, even possible inheritance. Also, victory after struggle.

Contingent upon where this card falls, there are new foundations entering the individual's life

Finally, joy. The child you were still resides in you and must be cared for.

Reversed

Reversed, this card signifies someone who is generous with love and affection, and, at times can be naive. This individual might unrealistically have ideas about love, relationships and marriage.

Reversed, it also means that the individual is feeling that they have missed out on a contented and loving childhood. Encountered grave complications at a young age. An unhappy home life. An abusive parent. Child abuse. Family rifts and problems.

Living in the past instead of the present. Yearning for a past that will never return.

Contingent upon the way it falls, these individuals grip to the past and outmoded habits.

VII of Cups

Meaning Upright

This card specifies that we are faced with a time of decision, that the imageries we see must be fixed whether in dreams or the world of reality. As you can see, the person in this card is a fantasist who is able to see beauty and enthusiasm as well as dreadful trials and complications in the future. If we are continually trapped in our dreams, or fears, we will never be able to move forward.

A choice needs to be made no matter what.

This card talks of letting go of a former relationship, job or project. It is vital to look wisely at how chaotic your situation has become.

This is a wish card. And, you can also see that there is a cup with a snake and a cup with a demon. This is displaying that wishes can go wrong. In reality, it can be a blessing. Be cautious what you wish for, you might get it, but with a price.

This card can also refer to a boundless mystical experience that the individual has gone through or is going to go through.

Reversed

Good use of purpose and will. This card, reversed, might show a reluctance to deal with the reality of life, a warning to get your head out of the clouds. It can also tell that this individual depends on false hope rather than reality.

Contingent upon where it falls, it can mean indecision means lost opportunities.

VIII of Cups

Meaning Upright

Overstretching yourself to the point of collapse. This card warns the individual to slow down before he/she gets totally burned out. Denunciation of material life and dissatisfaction in love.

It is a card representative of withdrawal, self-pity, over-giving, over-extending.

This individual uses too much carefulness, not enough belief, and has misgivings about success. They waver to think positively.

This card shows a new path in life is what is being sought by this individual.

Follow your heart. Take a break and create change.

In a relationship reading, this card highlights that you would preferably like to escape the emotional problems that surround the relationship and continue as if you were in a perfect relationship. Yet, you know that these matters will continue to plague the relationship if unaddressed.

Reversed

Jealousy is present. A message you have been waiting for has yet to come. Do not turn out to be too brave or to daring.

Business will slow down for you, and your love life will be at a standstill. In reverse, this card says that somebody has abandoned something which was well-established for an impossible dream.

It also suggests the individual is uncontrolled and fidgety.

IX of Cups

Meaning Upright

The IX of Cups shows good health and lots of success. There will be a state of affairs which will offer your best interests. Material gains might be part of your realization as well as emotional support in life. Your work will begin optimistic, then turn dark, and then be optimistic again. Don't worry, after a minor retrograde, you will see material gain or a decent result. An emotional matter regarding the care or treatment of another will be debated.

Nines signify individual honor and conclusion, or the ending stage of growth. Nine is connected with the Moon - thus dreams and delusions play a role in cards numbered nine. This last stage might bring certain complications with it, and past experiences and means of coping become significant here and are an inherent part of the meaning devoted to the nines.

The Nine of Cups signifies self-actualization, solidity and progression. It signifies success, triumph, and financial well-being. This card indicates gratification of good personal relationships, love and friendship, as well as contented material situations are shown. It is a card that mirrors happiness in health, finances, work, luck, love or relationship.

This is the traditional wish card, so whatever the individual wishes can be theirs. However, everything comes with a price, and they need to be cautious what they wish for due to the fact that they are very likely to receive it!

Reversed

Reversed, it proposes that you might be upset that your desires are not materializing. Maybe there are lots of wishes that you have, but there is some frustration because these aren't being rewarded.

Reversed, it can also point to displeasures due to deficiencies and errors, complacency, greed, gluttony, shallow or materialistic morals and extreme obsession with satisfying your own wishes, often times at the expense of others.

It can also specify ill-fortune due to overindulgence in food, alcohol, or drugs and the costs that come with it.

Reversed, this card also points to a request that is not yet satisfied, possibly because it is wanted too strongly or the individual is damaging their own hard work. At time, this card will show up reversed when the individual is going through a depression or lack of self-esteem.

X of Cups

Meaning Upright

The X of Cups is revealing a good family life. Happiness, joy and serenity will rule your life. There will be communication associated with your work that will encompass mail, phone calls, or special application. You will get a long-distance phone call from a relative, or you will make one.

The X of Cups signifies the sustaining contentment of love in a relationship with another. This card is very positive with regard to relationships and might show either the beginning of a new, happy relationship, or the definitive gratification of a long-term relationship.

Success. You must be more conscious of how successful and esteemed you truly are.

This is a card representative of long-lasting happiness and security.

The individual has a good character.

Reversed

Reversed, this card shows either a family squabble or a loss of friendship. Chance of unfaithfulness. Young people might turn against their parents. Someone manipulates the social order for private gain.

Reversed, it can also show an abrupt vicious explosion of a well-organized environment or well-organized routine. It specifies that someone has anti-social movements.

Page of Cups

Meaning Upright

Good Looking. Studious, loving, might be an individual with a young frame of mind. Supportive, dependable, but not strong. They offer service and want to be of help.

This individual is interested in poems and the arts, dreamy sometimes, yet brave when bravery is needed.

This card shows news, maybe of a birth. Somebody is emotionally weak and desires love. The dynamism of this card is nearly always tender and youthful. The essence of this card is of ingenuity and feelings.

In a reading concerning spiritual matters, the Page could specify the start of a spiritual journey commenced for emotional motives.

It can mean a time is required for silent reflection.

Also, this individual is very educated and gives it away without restrictions.

Reversed

Reversed, it shows someone who is adolescent or has emotional difficulties. It can portray an individual who is evading reality thru drugs or alcohol, or somebody who is running from the truth. This is an individual who is expressively uncertain and incapable of conducting good relationships. He/she expects too much and doesn't give enough. He/she is deficient in the areas of egotism and self-acceptance, and might be emotionally offensive. This individual has widespread and unfocused emotions, and might thus imagine a lot and get their feelings hurt without reason. He/she is mistrustful, self-doubting, hypocritical, egotistical and easily depressed. Little to no desire to create.

Knight of Cups

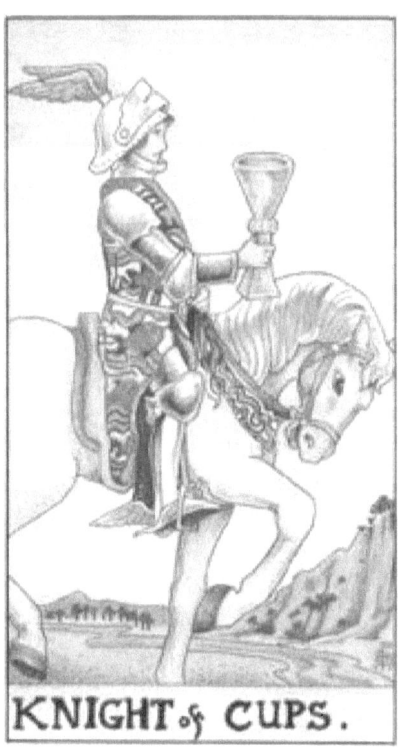

Meaning Upright

Might be a traveler. Enthusiastic, amiable and often lyrical and elegant.

The Knight of Cups signifies the coming of somebody or something. An invite or request might be received. A proposal might be made on behalf of somebody else thru a 3rd party.

Expect constructive changes since things are looking up.

Cups mean emotions. The Knight is looking toward his emotions to deliver a map. He is the individual who is governed by his heart as opposed to his head. When needing to make a decision, this individual always goes with what his/her heart is telling him/her, whether rational or not. High intelligence. Romantic dreamer. If a woman, she may be falling in love with a man of this type. The young man is friendly. A messenger.

This card signifies change and exciting news.

Reversed

Reversed, this individual allows their emotions too much control. They might be temperamental, envious and/or emotional to point of ineffectiveness. He/she might jump to assumptions prior to receiving all the facts.

Reversed, it is telling to either look at yourself and how you are acting, or understand that the individual might be acting from his/her emotions rather than logic.

The Knight of Cups reversed shows a state of affairs which was primarily very alluring, dreamy and exhilarating, but which later turns out to be something quite different.

Be wary of deception and fraud.

Queen of Cups

Meaning Upright

The Queen of cups is warm, loving, outgoing, pleasant, dedicated, truthful, compassionate, friendly, artistically gifted and imaginative.

The Queen of Cups is adored and admired for her fairmindedness and honesty. She is warm-hearted and a virtuous friend. She shows that a woman might support you in your circumstances. This card shows a nurturing personality. She sincerely cares about the well-being of others. She can be a mother, or a mother figure.

The Queen gives at will to others. She is highly intuitive. You might be called upon to help another. You will be glad to do so, but be sure to take care of yourself also.

Pay close consideration to your inner voice, and trust your intuition. You may feel a spurt of inspiration, or become involved in an inspired venture.

This is a happy card that signifies stability and harmony. It also specifies success that is attained due to decent imagination.

Reversed

Reversed, it indicates that your imagination runs away with you. You mean well, but can't be relied upon. An undependable woman may be near. This person is out of touch with feelings, overcome by emotions, nervous, unbalanced, gloomy, distrustful, erratic, indecisive, temperamental, unprofessional, disloyal, self-indulgent, excessively secretive, cold and manipulative, illogical, gossiper, hurts others, stubborn, hostile, incapable of relating to children, unable to nurture. This individual changes feelings and opinions without cause.

King of Cups

Meaning Upright

The King of Cups is a business man in an authoritative position. A kindhearted nobleman, a paternal figure.

You might not understand him, but you can trust him. He has accomplished something in life and is sociable, loving and deep. He possesses intelligence combined with strong instinct. He also enjoys the comforts in life.

The King of cups has a love of arts and is responsible and generous.

He is the master of his own emotional state, and remains in control. The King of Cups embodies the balance between emotions and intellect.

The King is a man of business, law or spirituality. He is involved in the arts and sciences and relishes in quiet power. It can signify that somebody shows paternalistic feelings to you.

If there were a crisis, we should hope to have this individual near.

This is the kind of man that commands respect but not love. He is a natural-born manipulator and has attained his position in life by the use of his wits, not his strength. He evades taking individuals into his confidence and chooses to work in secret instead. He desires power, and is motivated by unseen reasons. Individuals both fear and distrust him.

Reversed

A powerful man, but he is most likely double dealing. A violent nature. A scandal is brewing so be cautious. This card signals somebody who is unsympathetic, corrupt, unrefined, brutal, self-doubting, juvenile, dull, untrue friend, useless advice, con artist, deceiving, deceitful, play acting, doubtful, lazy, exploitive, violent and traitorous ruler. This man has no morals and his only loyalty is to himself.

Chapter 7: The Minor Arcana - Pentacles

The Pentacles in the Tarot deck characterize material possessions, trade, business, finances, and security. They deal with the outward level of awareness.

Pentacles reflect the outer circumstances of your well-being, finances, work and imagination.

Pentacles Taurus, Virgo, and Capricorn.

Ace of Pentacles

This card is typically seen with a garden or agricultural backdrop to highlight its connection to Earth. The potential of getting this card is to serve as a seed of future contentment. In other words, if your gifts are established and tended to vigilantly, this seed will grow and reward you with a respectable yield. The Ace embodies the initial phase of your goal. You should repeat that phase so that it can cover boundless distances. This card represents a message of sustenance, and recommends that you move slowly, progressively, and with purpose in order to reach your long-standing goals.

Two of Pentacles

This card has an image of a man juggling with 2 Pentacles flying about in a figure-eight manner. What this means is that until one or the other Pentacle falls, an ultimate decision can't be made. There is more to learn prior to action being taken. Thus, the Two of Pentacles advises patience. Don't permit conditions to jostle you. You have plenty of time to work everything out, regardless of how vital things seem now. When this card appears, it shows that changes are coming, so remember to remain calm until you have all the information you need.

Three of Pentacles

This card is the card of intellect. It frequently portrays a leading craftsman looking to his colleagues for advice on how to complete a work of genius. Sometimes, the genius is represented alone in an inspired excitement. When the Three of Pentacles appears in your reading, it is a message to relish in all that you do, and to remain focused on the task you are currently working on. Thru realistic plans, teamwork, and a devotion to improvement, you will turn your dreams into truths.

Four of Pentacles

This card signifies the absurdity of material security, the disingenuous realism that comes when you have been well supported and protected, even though this affluence brings the burden of big choices and responsibilities. The Four of Pentacles wishes you to implement skills to wisely handle your funds and your situation, and to not be intimidated by surprise changes. When this card comes up in a reading, it is a note to make thorough decisions. Separate your self-esteem from your material value. You may be gripping, trying to keep control, and would profit by letting go of your attachment to your assets and other worldly worries; these are not the ways to true serenity.

Five of Pentacles

This card is the card of longing and fulfilment. Doing something for temporary fulfilment will frequently lead to enduring discontent. When money and achievement are your main focus, any impediment can bring an excessive upset to your honor. Or perhaps you have mistreated individuals in your life who were actually the ones who assisted you to get where you are, and now you leave them feeling hopeless and without help. Don't let money be your whole life. This card reminds you that treasures come in countless forms.

Six of Pentacles

This card is one of support and kindness. The Six of Pentacles is about giving and receiving, and the sense of balance that must be learned amongst the two. Know that when you give your time, cash, information or support to others in need, you are essentially paying back the universe for the periods where you received help in the past. In addition, you are opening the frequencies to receive assistance in the future. Similarly, when you are getting help from someone in your time of need, the message from this card is that you should be paying forward the same kindness when able in order to continue the karmic cycle.

Seven of Pentacles

This card is about doing the work that is essential. The notion of the Seven of Pentacles is cultivation. You should adopt the attitude that "slow and steady wins the race." The message contained within this card is to finish what you started. Despite how exasperating it might get, have tolerance and be self-assured in your hard work. When this card comes up in your reading, it is a reminder that the more attentive you are, the more likely you are to receive the results you desire.

Eight of Pentacles

This card is one of work and enhancement. You will notice the successful craftsperson working at his bench. Nonetheless, the Eight of Pentacles is not only based on getting the job done, it is also about doing the job well, and repeatedly looking for ways to progress and polish any specifics. However, with all this effort, there is always the risk of becoming an overachiever, and feeling so necessary that you will not ask for assistance or delegate any portion of a given project. When this card comes up in a reading, it inspires you to stay in your present mission or schooling, but to put energy into upholding a more well-adjusted life and outlook.

Nine of Pentacles

This card signifies monetary security, independence, achievement, and individuality. The woman on this card is able to endure her wealth and live a life of relaxation and extravagance, but only through much work, time, and expense. When this card appears in a reading, it means you should ensure that you are harmonizing your own hard work with time out and reward. Your message is to live self-assuredly, act graciously, and make your needs a precedence.

Ten of Pentacles

This card signifies the ending outcome of longstanding hard work that end in prosperity, wealth, legacies, and accomplishment. The Ten of Pentacles is a card of boundless achievement and pride, and can be an indicator of retirement, bequest, investments, and coziness later in life. But this card is also about family. It embodies close family ties and the affluence and knowledge that are passed down through generations. If the Ten of Pentacles appears in your reading, it is a cue to think long-term, and safeguard that your choices will get you nearer to your goals.

Page of Pentacles

This card represents a pupil of richness. His devotion is fixated on learning how to increase, grow, and cultivate his wealth. He watches individuals around him, learning from their faults and mentorship, become proficient at his own skills along the way. When the Page of Pentacles comes up in a reading, it means you should do your research. In other words, take a class, talk to somebody with knowledge; learn how to increase what you want in order to develop and endure your affluence. Know that this is not a time of act and accomplishment, but rather it is a time of groundwork and schooling.

Knight of Pentacles

This card is the most peaceable of all the Knights, the administrator of fruitfulness and growing. He moves at the frequency of the flow because he knows that you cannot rush time. Seeing the larger image, much like an agriculturalist preparing for forthcoming years, the Knight of Pentacles is systematic, devoted, and well-organized. His message is to be hands-on and persevere in your hard work. The work will not always be glitzy, but your honor rests on the obligation and follow-through, and your effort will be rewarded.

Queen of Pentacles

This card is filled with vast good sense and problem-solving dynamism. The Queen of Pentacles loves to counsel, inspire, foster, and empower those she is involved with, helping to resolve their problems. She is a teacher and a healer, and is pleased when sharing her time, liveliness, services, and money with others. If this card appears in a reading, it means to give of yourself, and concentrate on producing a relaxed, rich atmosphere for yourself and your loved ones. Practice being grounded in kindness. Or, in the interim, search for guidance from somebody in your life who displays these talents.

King of Pentacles

This card represents somebody who has achieved much in life and has a lot to show for it. The King of Pentacles is a creator who succeeds and a high-roller. He has boundless financial influence and reaps much admiration. This card represents reaching the top of the ladder, and maturing, not only profits, but also personal values. In a reading, the King of Pentacles embodies accomplishment and conclusion of longstanding goals. It is a reminder to work meticulously, and take the sturdiest, most dependable path to get where you are attempting to be in life. And once you get there, attempt to go even further.

Chapter 8: The Minor Arcana - Swords

Swords signify the East or North. They represent action, transformation, power, drive, domination, motivation, bravery, distress, and conflict. The swords deal with the intellectual level of awareness. Swords reflect the quality of mind existing in your thoughts, attitudes, and principles.

Should the Swords be high in a reading, you may assume that the individual has many decisions to make.

Ace of Swords

This card signifies your main purpose or guiding model, or the idea that leads you. It is a hopeful sign of development, growth, optimism, and triumph. This card might come up when you are at the start of a new project and are in need of further lucidity or strength to move ahead. The Ace of Swords delivers a message that basically means that you have the strength needed to handle everything that comes your way.

Two of Swords

This card is one of decision-making. It signifies differing ideas which need to be fixed in order to reach a happy place. If the Two of Swords comes up, it means that the person might be having to deal with countless mixed signs and misinterpretations, leaving them uncertain of which route to choose. In order to release yourself from this, this card wishes you to obtain as much info as you can so that you can contemplate all of it and make the best possible decision for your future.

Three of Swords

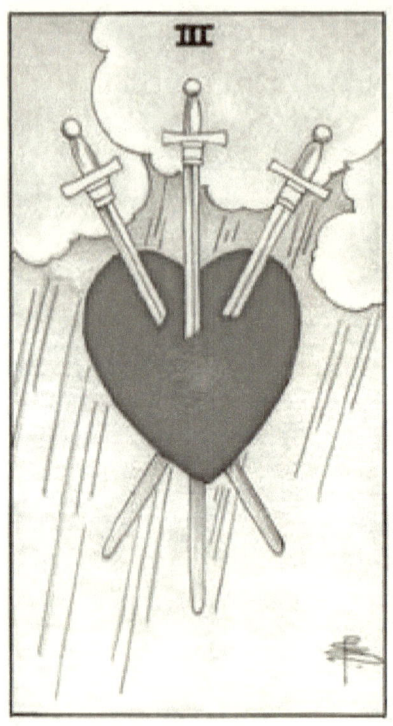

This card is one of the most identifiable. The Three of Swords shows sorrow, separation, and grief. While it may be cautioning you of imminent heartbreak, it frequently comes up when you are already in a place of anguish. This card can be painful, but it is encouraging you to lean into the pain and really experience and recognize it. Moving thru your emotions, as opposed to avoiding them, will give you the gift of strength, truth, healing, and growing.

Four of Swords

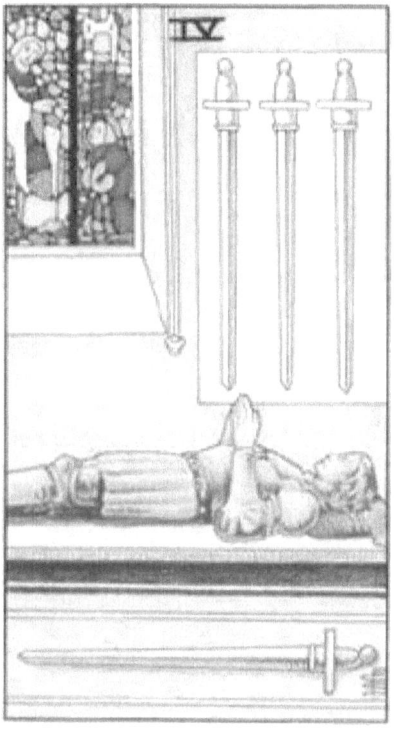

This card is encouraging you to take time out and go to a place of respite and tranquility. This is necessary in order to prevent yourself from reaching a state of overall emotional and physical burnout. If the Four of Swords appears in a reading, it basically means that you need a break. If you take this advice, you will move onward stronger, more whole, and more able, but only if you permit yourself time to stop and consider where you have been, and where you are going.

Five of Swords

This card is one of struggle, tension, winning, and losing. It is asking you to observe the cost of the fight you are partaking in. In other words, if you win the fight but lose friends, do you truly win? If the Five of Swords comes up in a reading, you should start thinking about what you are fighting for. Choose your battles intelligently. Otherwise, if you grasp that you may not have what it takes to fight the existing battle, do what you need to in order to be stronger next time. Think before you act.

Six of Swords

This card means leaving behind a particularly tough circumstance. This might feel very painful, and you might experience anxiety or remorse. However, if you want to move forward in life, you must leave something behind. If the Six of Swords appears in your reading, it is a helpful message of individual development, and a cue that, in the end, leaving this behind will open you up to something new. You will eventually look back and understand that you made the correct decision.

Seven of Swords

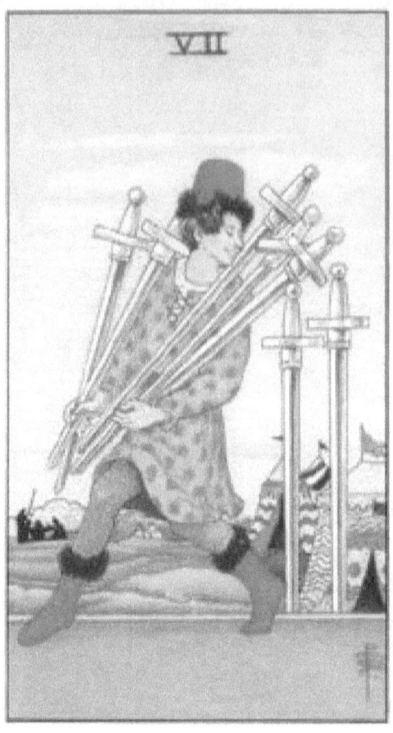

This card signifies trickery. It also inspires you to search for smart ways to climb ahead. The Seven of Swords is a prompt to work shrewder, not more. Nevertheless, the Seven of Swords is also hefty with disloyalty, and could show that you are the prey of someone else's secrets or trickery. Be on guard, and do not have faith in anything without asking questions first.

Eight of Swords

This card signifies the times in life when it feels like there is no way out. You feel trapped, bound and stuck. But you need to know that there is always a way out. When this card comes up in a reading, it is telling you that the way out is through your mind. What is holding you back is self-imposed. In other words, you are the one who made yourself the victim of your own restrictions, fears, expectations, and mentalities. If you want to be free, you are the only one who can set yourself free. The Eight of Swords' message is to either open your mind to a new outlook, or else remain stuck where you are.

Nine of Swords

This card is one of worry and anxiety. You are literally losing sleep keeping yourself full of worry. You may possibly feel helpless, like you have lost control of yourself and your emotions. When is card appears in a reading, it is a reminder to you that much of your stress is simply made up in your mind. Worrying is not going to help the situation. In fact, it is only going to feed it. However, these anxieties will stop having power over you when you address them at their foundation.

Ten of Swords

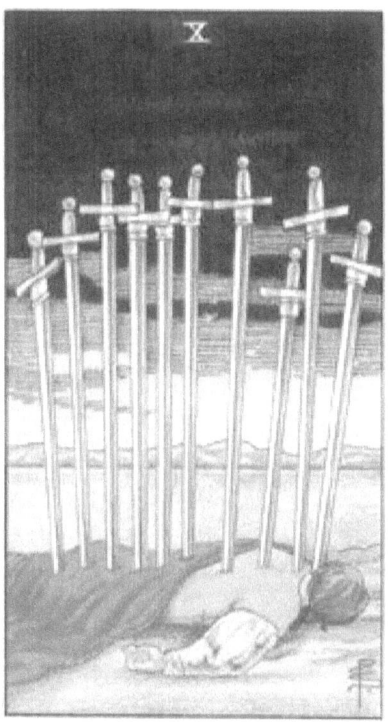

This card signifies conclusiveness. The boundary has been reached, a line has been crossed, and there is no turning back. In other words, the situation is over, and there is no hope for renewal. This might be seen as a heartbreaking loss, but often it will bring a sense of release and conclusion. Meaning, the waiting and pondering are over and there is no more uncertainty. If the Ten of Swords appears in your reading, let go and move on. There is no more improvement to be made.

Page of Swords

This card calls upon you to start your wheels in motion. You possess the passion you require, but there is much more info accessible to you which can significantly affect your achievement. If the Page of Swords appears in a reading, it means – perform your research, locate the facts, and come up with a strong proposal to move forward. There will be many tests on your path, and you will need to be equipped to move past them.

Knight of Swords

The Knight of Swords is prepared to go! He doesn't contemplate the costs and is not cautious of a contest. He is a shrill and agitated soul who shoots first and queries later. When this card appears in a reading, it means you should pause to focus yourself prior to moving forward. Think to yourself - are my intents good? Are my actions fair? A little consideration can keep you from running around pointlessly and aid in guiding you down the correct path.

Queen of Swords

The Queen of Swords is well aware of what she wants. She is clever, truthful, self-sufficient, and sovereign. She is not a conformer and is too intelligent to be limited to outdated roles. When this card shows up in a reading, it is a message to act with individuality and fight for yourself. In other words, never let anyone mold you into something you are not. Be stout and stand up for all that you are.

King of Swords

This card is a force of knowledge. The King of Swords doesn't convey an emotional air. His strong points are in the mind, intellect, truth, and justice. The King has expanded his knowledge thru experience. He approaches life in an impartial means which gathers admiration from those around him. While the King might appear casual or disconnected, he offers much support. When the King of Swords appears in a reading, you might be in the situation of giving direction to others, or could profit from requesting advice yourself. When you search for direction from this card, you will receive the truth.

Chapter 9: Performing and Understanding the 3 Card Tarot Spread

I'm a visual person, and I therefore elect to have the arrangement of the cards in a structure that will direct the way that I process the info in the reading.

That is why I believe that the construction of the reading creates better meaning in the reading. So, if I'm performing a reading regarding a relationship, I want it to be balanced to mirror the individuals who are present. Know that you will most likely find that the pictorial nature of your spread is what will make it most helpful. In a 3 Card Spread, the power is not necessarily in the assigned meaning by the order the cards are drawn, but also in the location of the cards. This is what helps me to instinctively sense the meaning within them.

Below is an example of a typical 3 Card Spread to get you started:

Typical 3 Card Spread

Card 1: The Past

The notion of the past naturally sounds obvious, but it doesn't necessarily mean that things took place long ago. It could be a discussion that took place just last week. In the above spread, the past is signified by The Hermit upright. When this card appears this way in a reading, it basically means that you will receive insight from the Divine or spirit world. The Hermit reminds us that our goals can be reached, but that the journey on the way there may not be easy.

Card 2: The Present

The card in the middle represents the present. Due to the fact that this spread holds only 3 cards, several things can be read into it that would typically be seen in several cards in larger spreads. It could mean how others interpret the circumstances, outside influences, unseen difficulties, etc. You will learn to interpret in your own way. Here we see a Five of Wand reversed. This shows that there is some disharmony going on currently, and you will need time and patience to get through and fix it.

Card 3: The Future

The final card signifies the future or the ultimate outcome. Depending on the situation or the question the individual is asking, it may be a long-term goal or a resolution. The 3rd card in this spread is the Ten of Cups, which means that long-standing relationships will flourish. It could denote a new home, or simply a new beginning. Look at the image on the card. It is about cheerfulness, dreams being fulfilled, and long-term happiness.

The pattern of your 3 Card spreads are completely up to you. It really does not matter, whatever you are comfortable with, as long as you have determined what each spot will mean. So, you to choose what you want the spread to look like:

- horizontal
- stepped
- vertical
- triangle
- two uprights and one bridging horizontal

Chapter 10: Performing and Understanding the Celtic Cross Spread

Are you interested in the Celtic Cross Spread? Know that it is one of the most frequently used, but is also one of the toughest to read correctly.

This spread is commonly used by beginners, but many tend to miss the more profound visions that are presented in this intricate spread.

If you wish to be a top-notch tarot reader using this spread, you're going to need to master the dynamic forces among the cards.

I will show you the arrangement of the spread and the basics of reading the relationships between the cards in the Celtic Cross spread.

Next is an example of a typical Celtic Cross Layout:

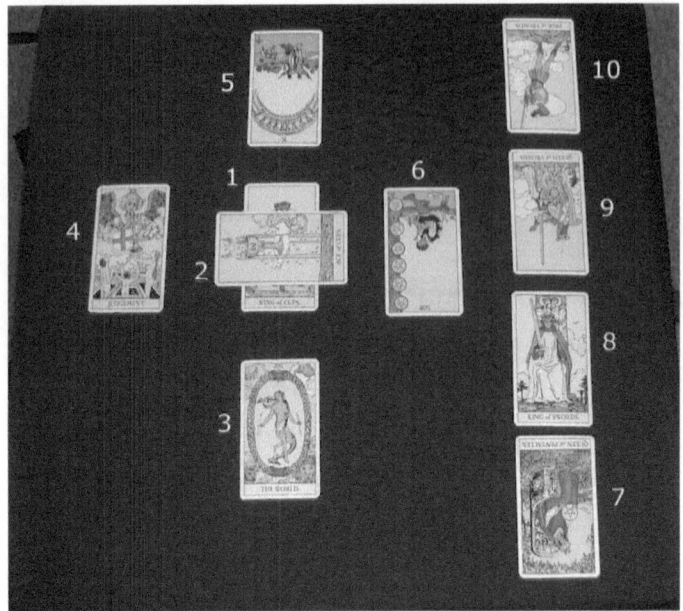

Card 1: The Querent

The Querent is the person in question, and that is what this card represents. Normally it is for the person themselves, but at times communications will come thru which is relevant to somebody in the individual's life instead. Therefore, if you find that the individual being read does not feel the meaning applies to them, it is more likely that it might be for a loved one.

Card 2: The Situation

This card specifies the current situation, or an upcoming situation. Always remember that this card might not relay to the question the individual is asking, but instead the question they should have asked. It usually means that there is an opportunity to solve a problem, or that difficulties are forthcoming.

If there is a challenge to be handled, this is frequently where it will appear.

Card 3: The Foundation

This card specifies issues that are in the past for this person, typically things from the very distant past. This card is a foundation that the state of affairs can be built upon.

Card 4: The Recent Past

This card shows proceedings that are much more current. It is regularly related to Card 3, but not always. For instance, if Card 3 showed monetary difficulties, Card 4 may display that the individual being read lost their job. In the interim, if the reading is positive, Card 4 may echo joyful proceedings that have taken place lately.

Card 5: Short-Term Outlook

This card specifies proceedings that will more than likely happen in the near future, probably in the next couple of months. It displays how the event will progress over the short term.

Card 6: Current State of an Issue

Card 6 shows us whether or not an issue is headed towards being resolved, or has festered. Always remember though that this card does not conflict with Card 2, which is merely letting us know whether or not there is a solution. This card tells us where the individual is with regard to the forthcoming result.

Card 7: Outside Influences

Card 7 shows how the Querent's friends and family really feel about the circumstances. It says that there are outside influences that might have an effect on the wanted outcome. And, even if those influences aren't affecting the outcome, they need to be considered when it is time to make a decision.

Card 8: Internal Influences

Card 8 will tell you what the Querent's true feelings are with regard to the situation at hand. Our internal feelings have a solid impact on our actions and deeds. At this time in the spread, take a look back at Card 1. Make a comparison of these two cards. Are there differences between them? If so, it may be likely that the individual's subconscious is working against them. For instance, if the reading is relative to a love affair, the individual may want to be with his/her lover, but feels he/she really needs to work things out with his/her spouse.

Card 9: Hopes and Fears

Card 9, though not the same as 8, is very similar. Our hopes and fears are regularly disputed, and sometimes we hope for the exact same thing that we are actually afraid of. As in the previous example of the lover and spouse being torn apart, he/she may be hopeful that his/her spouse learns of the affair and leaves him/her. This hope is due to the fact that it will then lift the burden of responsibility from the Querent. On the other hand, though, he/she may fear the spouse finding out.

Card 10: Long-Term Outcome

Card 10 discloses the probable long-term outcome of the issue at hand. Frequently, Card 10 characterizes the culmination of the other 9 cards together. The results can usually be noticed over the course of more than a few months all the way to a year. Sometimes Card 10 can be vague. When this happens, it's acceptable to pull 1 or 2 more cards, and look at them in the same position. At that point, it is likely that they will all link together to provide you with the perfect answer.

Now, I have taught you how the cards in the Celtic Cross Spread can prepare you for a successful reading, and then you turn that final card over, and you're not so sure.

You're thinking, "Did I do something wrong?" Doubtful.

What is most vital for you to remember is that reading Tarot cards is a progression of looking at somebody's else's life. However, always keep in mind that this is real life. It won't always end perfectly.

It is important for you to remember that you can inspire and tell positive outcomes in the cards, but you will be doing a disservice by not showing your clients all the options, which includes those that aren't so great. Always keep it real.

Chapter 11: Interpreting the Cards to Tell a Story

When reading a Querent, you will be most successful if you tell a story about what you are seeing in the cards. In other words, don't just say, "Well, you have a 10 of Cups here which means love and happiness. Then, you have a Queen of Wands, which means someone is fertile. And, the Empress means fertility and wealth. Blah blah blah..." Boring.

Instead, say it like this:

"Hmmm... it looks to me like you are surrounded by love. It appears like I am looking at a very happy relationship. Now, there's a woman in your life who is fertile... is someone trying to get pregnant? I ask you this because the Empress indicates fertility, and when she's paired up with that Queen..." and so on and so forth.

You see how making it an actually story is so much more interesting.

Be creative, and go! It's your time to do the best reading you can!

Chapter 12: Conclusion - An Easy Spread to Get You Started

So, now you should have adequate basic material from this book to use your new tarot deck. For simplification purposes, I will finish this book with a very easy spread to start you out on your readings.

As you probably have noticed, the tarot deck is very elaborate with connotation. I simply gave you the fundamentals.

When you perform a reading, you will see from the connotations of the cards that the connection between cards can get very involved and complex for a beginner.

The initial thing you can do to acquaint yourself with the cards as a daily exercise would be to shuffle the deck and pick one card for yourself. Ask the deck what is going on with you today, and then choose a card. When you choose the card, interpret it founded on how you feel. You actually just did a very simple reading for yourself. After doing this every day until you feel comfortable, you can now choose 3 cards.

3-card spreads are very beneficial and easy:

1. Shuffle the cards.

2. Focus on the question.

3. Put 1 card in the middle. Dependent upon your question, it can be any situation. It all depends on how you want to use the spread. This is the present.

4. The 2nd card that you will place on the left side is the past. This is what occurred prior to the card in the middle.

5. Next, place the 3rd card on the right side. That is the future

You just did your first reading! When you feel comfortable with 3 cards, you can move on to 4. Once you place your first card, you will place the 2nd card horizontally across it to make the shape of a cross. That signifies any impediment or thing that is hindering your state of affairs. The card meaning on the left remains the same, and the card on the right is the outcome or the future. You can also call card #1 the situation at hand, and the crossing card the hindrance.

I hope this book motivates you to go on to become a skilled tarot reader!

If you enjoyed learning about Tarot, I would be forever grateful if you could leave a review on Amazon. Reviews are the best way to help your fellow readers (both Tarot and otherwise) sort through the fluff and find the quality books. So, make sure to help your fellow readers out and Leave a Review. I would really appreciate it!

Also, if you learned and found this book useful, please share with your friends!

For more in-depth Tarot training, I can highly recommend The Ultimate Online Tarot Reading Course. This course includes extremely helpful videos to help master the meanings of each card and show you exactly how to do spreads correctly. You can check it out HERE With this course, you will be reading Tarot like a pro in no time!

www.ingramcontent.com/pod-product-compliance
Lightning Source LLC
Chambersburg PA
CBHW021149080526
44588CB00008B/267